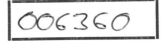

Ma Cuisine des Saisons

Georges Blanc

Translated and adapted by Caroline Conran

MACMILLAN
LONDON

First published in France 1984 by
Éditions Robert Laffont, S.A., Paris

This English translation first published 1987 by
MACMILLAN LONDON LIMITED
4 Little Essex Street London WC2R 3LF
and Basingstoke

Associated companies in Auckland, Delhi, Dublin, Gaborone,
Hamburg, Harare, Hong Kong, Johannesburg, Kuala Lumpur,
Lagos, Manzini, Melbourne, Mexico City, Nairobi, New York,
Singapore and Tokyo

British Library Cataloguing in Publication Data
Conran, Caroline
  Ma cuisine des saisons.
  1. Cookery, French
  I. Title II. Blanc, Georges
  641.5944   TX719

  ISBN 0-333-43206-1

Typeset by Bookworm Typesetting, Manchester
Printed in Hong Kong

Contents

A ma mère, à ma grand-mère, qui m'ont
guidé dans un métier que j'aime . . .

Introduction

Georges Blanc is owner, host and master-chef of the three-star Restaurant Georges Blanc, formerly La Mère Blanc, at Vonnas, near Bourg-en-Bresse. Approached through rolling green countryside and the flower-filled streets of small villages, less than an hour's drive from Lyons, the restaurant immediately exerts a powerful charm; it overflows with the well-being of a thoroughly well-run enterprise. This ambiance comes to a great extent from Monsieur Blanc himself; young, considerate, serious, he devotes himself heart, soul and guts to his work, and he has a deep love and respect for his *métier*. The restaurant itself, handsome, calm and comfortable, has the unintimidating air of a well-polished country house, and the food is extravagantly delicious. People often arrive at a three-star restaurant with over-inflated expectations, but here they are seldom, if ever, disillusioned.

Monsieur Blanc's approach to his art is well explained in his own introduction. The recommendations in his book are clear: cook with instinct, knowledge and dedication; taste and taste again; take pains over every dish – every time you make it, try to make it better. Often his recipes, although luxurious and lavish, are relatively simple and he has included perfected traditional and local dishes in the book, which he serves without elaboration: crying leg of lamb, frogs' legs sautéed with herbs, cherry clafoutis, braised beef with carrots, and calf's head – there are many examples of food that has the satisfying flavour which comes from generations of experience in the cooking of a dish.

Behind Maître Blanc, generations of good cooks are ranged. From his great-grandmother, his grandmother Elisa (the original Mère Blanc) and his mother Paulette, who took over the restaurant before the war, he has learned the art of cooking at first hand. Because of his background he has always known what good food should be and in his hands even the most inventive, up-to-the minute recipe – perhaps a soup of oysters with wild mushrooms – succeeds in having the satisfying flavour of truly good food.

When you live in the country the seasons are all important. They mean the flush of eggs, the quality of cream, the availability of asparagus, wild mushrooms or partridge. Georges Blanc likes to move with the seasonal changes; they are reflected in his menus and in the type of cooking – lighter in the summer, more comforting and substantial in the winter. So he has divided his book by seasons, to make sure that every dish is made to suit the weather and to ensure that the ingredients are at their peak of quality.

Monsieur Blanc's most important advice is to take infinite pains over the balance of each dish, using instinct and judgement rather than following the recipe unthinkingly, particularly where there is a sauce involved. There are no such things as exact measurements; the measuring is done by the palate and by the eye.

Actual techniques need constant attention too. The art of frying is something every cook has to learn. We all know that if you sauté meat or shellfish at too low a temperature at the start, all the juices will run out and boil rather than fry the food. On the other hand, as Monsieur Blanc points out, if you turn up the heat too high or for too long, you risk drying out the surface and making it hard. Attention and judgement are needed to find the right temperature and the exact moment to lower the heat, as soon as the surface is lightly seared, so that it remains golden, soft, glistening and lightly caramelised, and does not allow the escape of juices.

Another important aspect is the timing of roasting. Always use your judgement and test either by pressing steak, a piece of fish or a scallop with your finger, or in large joints of meat, birds, etc., by inserting a needle, to gauge whether it is just *à point*. This knowledge comes with experience, and by working at it an amateur can become an expert.

Living close to Bourg-en-Bresse, Monsieur Blanc is used to buying the most splendid poultry in the world. We can't buy Bresse chickens here very easily, but first-quality poultry, and also many of the difficult meats such as calf's head, calves' feet, sweetbreads and raw *foie gras* are available from La Boucherie Lamartine, 229 Ebury Street, London SW1, and they far outclass what is generally available. If you live further away, try to find free-range chickens or *poulets de grain* (maize-fed chickens with a yellow colour). They are firmer and have a little more flavour than the ordinary broiler.

Where Dublin Bay prawns are mentioned, he is referring to fresh Dublin Bay prawns (*Nephrops norvegicus*, also known as *langoustines* or scampi). Bought raw in their shells and cooked at home, they taste quite wonderful, sweet and succulent; freshly cooked by the fishmonger, they are still delicious. But freezing removes a lot of their flavour and spoils the texture as well. (Incidentally, not all shellfish sold as scampi are real Dublin Bay prawns, although they should be.) Where he mentions large Dublin Bay prawns, he means at least six inches long, with heads and claws. Very good ones, often from Scotland, can be ordered when they are available from La Marée, 76 Sloane Avenue, London SW3.

Freshwater crayfish are also hard to find, although our own chalk streams used to be full of them and in some places still are. However, you can sometimes obtain them from Richards (Soho) Ltd, 11 Brewer Street, London W1. Other sources are to be found through the British Crayfish Marketing Association, Riversdale Farm, Stour Provost, Gillingham, Dorset, or they can be ordered direct from Jane Oldry, Stanton Farm, Assington, Colchester,

Essex. The season starts on 1 July and runs to the end of November or thereabouts.

When you are using only the tails of the crayfish, Dublin Bay prawns or lobsters, it is worth reserving the heads and claws in the freezer to be used later in the making of shellfish sauce (p.17).

Vonnas lies in the Dombes, an area full of mysterious reedy lakes, home to various wildfowl, freshwater fish and frogs. Frogs' legs are one of the specialities of Georges Blanc's restaurant. To the British they still seem slightly exotic and buying them fresh is almost unheard of, but The London Larder, 4 Black Swan Yard, Bermondsey Street, London SE1, brings in fresh frogs once a week from France. Monsieur Blanc does not recommend frozen ones, since they tend to be dry and the juices are important to the finished dish.

The Ain, and Burgundy in general, is full of flowering meadows; dairy-farming is a major occupation, and the cooking at Vonnas reflects this and relies on quite lavish use of good white cream (not cream coloured as we like it in Britain) and very fresh, unsalted butter. The cream is usually *crème fraîche* and a recipe for making this can be found on p.23.

The stock used in sauce-making is always clarified stock, home-made and of good quality, but Monsieur Blanc allows that one can use stock cubes if no fresh stock is available – which makes life a lot easier.

On the whole this is an easy, relaxed book to use; most of the recipes are very accessible and none are over-complicated. The basic sauces, however, are very important and they appear frequently throughout the book. Mounting a sauce with butter, or making whisked butter (p.11) is not in fact very difficult, provided you whisk vigorously and do not have too much liquid to start off with. Practise with water and butter and you will quickly find the knack.

In one or two sauces *beurre manié* – equal amounts of flour and softened butter worked to a paste – is used as an emulsifier. There is no taboo on flour, and traditionally it has always been used. I personally think that the ritual exclamations of horror that go up whenever flour is mentioned are misguided – why should flour be more fattening or indigestible in a sauce than it is in pastry? If used with judgement it can make all the difference between a well-balanced, well-flavoured, light, velvety sauce, which complements a dish and one which has to be reduced and reduced to obtain the correct texture and which is then too rich and heavy-flavoured (and quite often too salty).

Of course, adding too much flour, like too much of anything, can spoil a dish, but Georges Blanc uses it, as did his mother and grandmother, with good instinct and good judgement – the two qualities which are his hallmarks and which make this book such a pleasure to use.

Caroline Conran

3

From Mother to Son

I owe my first gastronomic experiences to my grandmother Elisa. She had retired to her little cottage, just opposite our house, and on Thursdays, or in the evenings after school, I would run over to see her and enjoy her memorable cream caramel flavoured with vanilla. On top of that, my grandfather Tisseraud made the most delicious sweet, cream-filled tarts at his bakery and pastry-shop in the church square.

At that time, like my son Alexander who is now the same age as I was then, I preferred sweet things to the little fried fish caught by our old gardener and odd-job man Jean-Marie, but my keenest pleasure was to go with him to the banks of the Renon to try for gudgeon, or to cast his nets into the river Veyle. He knew by instinct exactly where to find the pike, carp and turbot which my grandmother cooked, quite simply, in foaming *beurre noisette*. But when it came to eating, it was, as it is with all children, sweet things that got my palate going and I think it was the taste of my first caramel that gave me the burning ambition to cook.

Later, as son, grandson and great-grandson of a line of cooks, I could feel, when I stood in front of the stoves of the family inn and when I served my very first guests, the force of my inheritance. The generations that preceded me in this old house left such a strong impression that I could only follow them. My enthusiasm grew to a passion to hand down their message.

The three cooks before me had always cooked lovingly, simply and with total honesty. Their repertoire was limited but it used to best advantage all the local produce, which was chosen with care and was always of a quality that was beyond reproach. Their skill, their judgement of seasoning, their exact timing and their knowledge of what will please and satisfy the palate brought them fame and fortune. Since then cooking has evolved into something different; some people talk, rightly, of the *nouvelle cuisine*, and the chefs of today have created new tastes and new pleasures.

In the old days the produce was grown naturally, without the help of chemicals. Cultivation and the rearing of stock can now be artificially forced, cutting costs but impairing the quality at the same time. So nowadays looking for really high-class ingredients is more important and more taxing than ever.

Today, cooking is lighter than before, more natural and freer, with unending possibilities for invention, improvisation and self-expression. Over-rich and over-elaborate classical cuisine has given way to dishes that rely on the rhythm of the seasons and the resources of the local countryside. They are simply cooked with great precision and attention to detail,

5

seasoning and tasting and timing, to obtain a result that is perfectly balanced, with a faultless blending of flavours.

To make a good sauce, which is the essence of French cooking, one must always be a perfectionist, tasting and tasting again and using the different ingredients imaginatively, like a musician with his instrument or an artist with his palette of colours. This is the way to find the depth of flavour that makes a good sauce perfect. This seeking for perfection means adding a sharp note with a dash of vinegar or white wine or lemon, a heightened taste with a pinch of spice; it is increasing the unctuosity of a sauce with a little olive oil or a nut of butter, or bringing out a fresh flavour at the last moment with a handful of chopped herbs.

Constantly changing, the new cooking also has to flatter the eye to satisfy today's gourmets, who are avid for new experiences and enjoy the new freedom. But the new ways must still respect and draw a lesson from the teaching of the past.

Cooking in its highest form is often compared to other major arts – architecture, painting or sculpture – but unlike them it produces only ephemeral works, conceived, created and appreciated in a few short moments . . . they survive only in people's memories. So a cook must have plenty of humility and perhaps a certain amount of trepidation as he approaches his daily task of creating and recreating something as precisely as if it were a lithograph or a piece of music.

If there is a career which has a lifelong apprenticeship, it is certainly ours; the desire to obtain more profound results all the time keeps our passion alive. But to be a cook right through to the soul, and to be skilful in practice, is still not enough. In addition, the art of making a simple meal into a celebration is vital, even if the quality of the meal is irreproachable. You must know how to offer the gourmet the right surroundings and conditions to enjoy himself. Like a backdrop in the theatre, the décor forms an essential part of the occasion. So it is necessary to establish a pleasing and harmonious atmosphere; it lies in the way the table is set out, in the flowers, the antiques and furniture that stand about the room, the colours, the pictures and the lighting – everything reflecting the personality and feelings of the host.

Happy and successful cooking doesn't rely only on know-how; it comes from the heart, makes great demands on the palate and needs enthusiasm and a deep love of food to bring it to life.

In the following chapters you will find a selection of family and local recipes, mixed with my own ideas. I have tried to alternate elaborate gourmet recipes, ideal for celebrations, with good everyday recipes using humble ingredients.

I hope when you cast your eye over these pages that they will make you want to try them out and give you the means of succeeding.

Georges Blanc

6

Editor's Note

The recipes in this book are grouped according to their seasonal character – Spring, Summer, Autumn and Winter. Within each season, dishes are divided into four sections – cold starters, warm starters, main courses and desserts.

Each recipe is graded according to:

Difficulty

♨ *easy*

♨ ♨ *more complicated*

♨ ♨ ♨ *elaborate*

Overall preparation and cooking time

◙ *less than 30 minutes*

◙ ◙ *30 minutes – 1 hour*

◙ ◙ ◙ *more than 1 hour*

Expense

£ *inexpensive*

£ £ *moderately expensive*

£ £ £ *expensive*

Basic
Preparations

Emulsified Butter Sauces

Beurres émulsionnés

Classic Beurre Blanc *(Beurre blanc classique)*
Preparation time – 15 minutes

125g *(4¹/₂ oz)* butter, softened
3 tablespoons white wine vinegar
3 tablespoons water
3 shallots, peeled
salt, freshly ground pepper

Chop the shallots very finely and throw them into a small saucepan with the vinegar and the water. Boil to cook the shallots and reduce the liquid. When the liquid has almost completely evaporated, put the pan over a bain-marie and incorporate the butter gradually, whisking over a very gentle heat.

When all the butter has been added, season the sauce with salt and pepper and strain it through a fine sieve (unless you want to keep the shallots in the sauce to give it a more rustic finish).

Beurre Blanc with Cream *(Beurre blanc crémé)*

This is made in the same way as the previous recipe, but when the reduction is complete 2 tablespoons of double cream or *crème fraîche* are added to the shallots, together with 2 tablespoons of vinegar and 2 of water. Allow the mixture to reduce a little more, then gradually incorporate the softened butter, finishing the sauce as before.

The addition of a little cream at this early stage in the recipe makes it possible to hold the sauce at a higher temperature without it separating, and it can therefore be served hotter. It also looks finer, both in colour and texture, and has an added sheen.

Whisked Butter *(Beurre battu)*

Cut 125g *(4¹/₂ oz)* of cold butter into small cubes with a kitchen knife and put them ready on a saucer. Keep them cool.

Heat 125ml *(4¹/₂ fl. oz)* of water in a small pan over a brisk heat. When it comes to the boil, gradually incorporate the cold butter, whisking it into the boiling liquid a little at a time.

Season with salt and a few drops of lemon juice. Keep warm in a bain-marie over a gentle heat.

Whisked butter can be used to finish various sauces, giving a good buttery flavour and a light texture, without adding too much in the way of animal fat.

Fresh Tomato Sauce 1

Concassé de tomates

For four people

Preparation time – 20 minutes

600g *(1 lb 5 oz)* ripe tomatoes, skinned, deseeded and diced
20g *(¾ oz)* butter
4 tablespoons olive oil
3 shallots, chopped
2 cloves of garlic, peeled
bouquet garni of 1 bay leaf, 2 sprigs of thyme, 2 sprigs of parsley, 1
    stick of celery and the green of 1 leek leaf
2 teaspoons tomato purée
1 lump of sugar
coarse salt, freshly ground pepper

Put the butter and oil in a saucepan and heat gently. Throw in the shallots and let them soften over a gentle heat until they are a pale golden colour. Add the diced tomatoes, garlic, *bouquet garni*, tomato purée and sugar. Cook gently for 20 minutes, remove the *bouquet garni* and garlic, season the sauce with salt and pepper and keep it ready for use.

Suggestions

This tomato sauce can be used in the making of various dishes to heighten the flavour at the end of the cooking by adding a sharp touch, and it pleases the eye with its vibrant colour.

Tomato Sauce 2

Coulis de tomates

For four people

Preparation time – 45 minutes

600g *(1 lb 5 oz)* ripe tomatoes, peeled, deseeded and coarsely
    chopped
20g *(¾ oz)* butter
4 tablespoons olive oil
3 shallots, finely chopped
2 teaspoons tomato purée
2 cloves of garlic, peeled
bouquet garni of 1 bay leaf, 2 sprigs of thyme, 2 sprigs of parsley, 1
    stick of celery and the green of 1 leek leaf
1 lump of sugar
coarse salt, freshly ground pepper

Put the butter and oil in a saucepan and heat gently. Throw in the shallots and
let them soften briefly over a gentle heat.

Add the tomato purée, stir, then immediately add the diced tomatoes, the 2
whole cloves of garlic, *bouquet garni*, salt, pepper and sugar. Bring to the
boil, stirring thoroughly, then cook, covered, for 30 minutes over a medium
heat.

When the sauce is cooked and reduced, remove the *bouquet garni* and cloves
of garlic. Purée the sauce in a food processor or liquidiser. If the sauce seems
too watery, reduce it again over a low heat. Taste for seasoning.

Suggestions

Tomato sauce can be used as the basis of several sauces, or as an additional
ingredient. According to your own ideas, you could add more olive oil, some
cream or a *beurre blanc* to take the edge off the sauce, or to make it smoother
and more velvety. You could heighten the flavour by adding small quantities
of fresh herbs such as chervil, tarragon or fresh thyme flowers, freshly
chopped.

Aromatic White Wine Court-bouillon

Court-bouillon vin blanc aux aromates

For four people

Preparation time – 15 minutes; cooking time – 30 minutes

1 bottle *(750ml)* dry white wine
500ml *(16 fl. oz)* water
1 onion, stuck with a clove
bouquet garni of sprigs of parsley, half a bay leaf and a sprig of thyme
3 shallots, peeled
2 cloves of garlic, peeled
2 sticks of celery
zest of half a lemon
coarse sea salt, freshly ground pepper

Put the white wine and water in a saucepan with all the vegetables and herbs and the lemon zest.

Boil rapidly for 30 minutes; halfway through the cooking, add 2 tablespoons of sea salt and a few turns of the peppermill.

At the end of the cooking time, strain through a fine sieve, allow to cool and keep in the refrigerator or cold larder for later use.

Suggestions

A basic ingredient in several of my sauces, this *court-bouillon* can be used for cooking all shellfish (particularly freshwater crayfish). It can also be added to a variety of sauces to give them both lightness and fluidity and to add a certain edge and vigour (but without acidity), which can help to give a dish character.

Sauce Aigrelette

Sauce aigrelette

For four people

Cooking time – 30 minutes

1 egg yolk
1 teaspoon mustard
4 tablespoons oil of arachide
2 tablespoons olive oil
2 tablespoons soya oil
1 tablespoon white wine vinegar
125ml *(14½ fl. oz)* aromatic white wine *court-bouillon* (p.14)
a squeeze of lemon juice
1 tablespoon each tarragon, chervil and chives, finely chopped
salt, freshly ground pepper

Make a mayonnaise in the usual way with the egg yolk, mustard and the different oils.

Then make the mayonnaise into a more fluid sauce by adding the white wine vinegar, *court-bouillon* and lemon juice. Stir in the fresh herbs and season with salt and pepper.

The sauce should be light and should not stick to the spoon. Vary the quantities of the various ingredients to change the character of the sauce.

Suggestions

This sauce can be used to dress cold entrées (such as salads of crayfish, scallops or frogs' legs). Warmed very slightly, it can also be served with steamed or poached fish. You could also add a generous tablespoon of whipping cream to the sauce, or colour it green with a tablespoon of spinach or watercress purée.

Georges Blanc's Sauce Marinière

Sauce marinière de Georges Blanc

For four people

Cooking time – 45 minutes

half a bottle *(375ml)* dry white wine
250ml *(9 fl. oz)* water

aromatics for the court-bouillon

2 carrots, peeled
1 onion, peeled
4 shallots, peeled
2 cloves of garlic, peeled
bouquet garni of half a bay leaf, 1 sprig of thyme, 1 bunch of
    parsley, 1 stick of celery
1 lemon, peeled

salt, freshly ground pepper

for the sauce

3 shallots, finely chopped
100ml *(4 fl. oz)* good quality olive oil
3 tablespoons fresh tomato sauce (p.12)
12 fresh thyme flowers, finely chopped
half a bay leaf, crushed
a squeeze of lemon juice

for finishing the sauce
juice of half a lemon
4 tablespoons water
120g *(4½ oz)* butter, chilled and cut into dice
3 tablespoons fresh chives, tarragon and basil, finely chopped
a few sprigs of chervil
salt, freshly ground pepper

Making the *court-bouillon*

Put the white wine and water in a saucepan with the aromatics for the *court-bouillon* and boil for 30 minutes. At the end of the cooking time, season with salt and pepper, strain and reserve.

Making the sauce

Soften the chopped shallots in the olive oil. Add the tomato sauce, chopped thyme flowers, crushed bay leaf and a squeeze of lemon juice, and allow to reduce for about 8 minutes. Remove the bay leaf.

Making the whisked butter and finishing the sauce

In a separate pan bring the lemon juice and 4 tablespoons of water to the boil and whisk in the butter, a little at a time. When the sauce is emulsified, remove it from the heat, season lightly and add it to the tomato sauce, followed by all the fresh herbs. You can play with the consistency of the sauce by adding more olive oil, more *court-bouillon* or more whisked butter. Whisk the sauce to a smooth consistency.

Suggestions

This sauce, not at all classic, is my own invention and is easily made by anyone who is a good judge of balanced flavours. Both eye and palate are important. To achieve a sauce with depth of flavour, character and *finesse*, experiment with the different elements, remembering the quantity you want to end up with.

This sauce should not be too liquid; it should be slightly velvety with a translucent sheen, set off by the fresh herbs and tomatoes.

Shellfish Sauce with Cream

Sauce coulis de crustacés à la crème

For four people

Cooking time – 45 minutes

1kg *(2¼ lb)* head shells from lobsters, crawfish or crayfish
80g *(3 oz)* butter
3 shallots, finely chopped
1 carrot, cut into thick slices
half a leek, sliced
1 bay leaf
a sprig of thyme
2 sprigs of tarragon
1 tablespoon cognac
1 litre *(1¾ pints)* double cream or *crème fraîche* (p.23)
salt, freshly ground pepper

Remove the gills from inside the head shells, as these can impart a bitter flavour to the sauce. Chop the shells into large pieces.

Heat the butter in a large pan over a brisk heat and brown all the vegetables and herbs, then add the shells and flame with the brandy.

Pour in the cream, season with salt and pepper and reduce over a moderate heat for half an hour. The cream will reduce by a third and develop a delicious flavour.

When it has reduced, strain the sauce, half at a time, through a fine wire sieve, pressing the shells well to extract all the juices. You should have a smooth, velvety, light and extremely well-flavoured sauce. Taste for seasoning.

Suggestions

This sauce can be used to prepare a *gratin* of freshwater crayfish or of seafood, a *bisque* of shellfish, and so on.

Beaujolais Sauce for Poultry

Sauce beaujolaise pour volaille

For four people

Preparation time – 1 hour

600g *(1 lb 5 oz)* chicken trimmings (wings, necks, carcasses, etc.)
100g *(3½ oz)* butter
2 tablespoons flour

flavourings for the reduction

1 carrot
1 onion
1 leek
4 shallots
1 stick of celery
3 cloves of garlic
2 bay leaves
a sprig of thyme
2 cloves

2 litres *(3½ pints)* strong red wine
500ml *(16 fl. oz)* veal stock (optional)
salt, freshly ground pepper

Chop the chicken trimmings and bones into large pieces and brown them in butter in a large saucepan. Add the flavourings and sprinkle with flour, stirring it in well.

Add the red wine, bring it to the boil and flame it; then add the veal stock, if you have it, to strengthen the flavour.

Season and leave to simmer gently for 1 hour. The sauce will reduce somewhat and develop its flavour. When it is a good consistency, strain through a fine wire sieve and reserve ready for use.

Foresters' Sauce

Sauce forestière

For four people

Preparation time – 30 minutes

250g *(8¹/₂ oz)* wild mushrooms (such as ceps, chanterelles or
    trompettes) or cultivated mushrooms, or a mixture of the two
20g *(³/₄ oz)* butter
2 shallots, chopped
500ml *(16 fl. oz)* double cream or *crème fraîche* (p.23)
2–3 tablespoons meat glaze (optional)
a squeeze of lemon juice
salt, freshly ground pepper

Wash the mushrooms carefully and blanch them in boiling salted water for 5 minutes. Drain them, then chop them in a food processor. Melt the butter in a saucepan and brown the shallots over a brisk heat, then add the mushrooms and pour in the cream.

Season with salt and pepper and simmer gently for about 10 minutes, until the sauce begins to emulsify.

Finish the sauce with a little meat glaze, if you have it, and add a squeeze of lemon juice to give it a bit of character.

Suggestions

This sauce can be served with a stuffed pigeon (p.168) or a roast joint (loin of lamb or a fillet of beef, for example). In this case, add some of the cooking juices to the sauce.

It is advisable not to chop the mushrooms too fine, or you will end up with a purée. The sauce should not be too thick. You can change its character in a variety of ways – by adding fresh herbs, a tablespoon of fresh tomato sauce (p.12) or perhaps a hint of garlic, some truffle juice or some chopped truffles if you are celebrating.

Bouillabaisse Sauce

Sauce bouillabaisse

For four people

Preparation time – 45 minutes

1.5kg *(3¹/₂ lb)* sea fish (hake, scorpion fish (rascasse), weaver,
    gurnard, whiting, etc.)
200ml *(7 fl. oz)* olive oil

flavourings for the basic stock
2 carrots
1 large onion, sliced
5 shallots, peeled
1 leek, cut into thick rounds
400g *(14 oz)* ripe tomatoes
2 tablespoons tomato purée
1 bay leaf
2 sprigs of thyme
a small bunch of parsley
2 sprigs of tarragon
a pinch of saffron
a pinch of cayenne
3 cloves of garlic
400ml *(14 fl. oz)* double cream or *crème fraîche* (p.23)
60ml *(2¹/₂ fl. oz)* whisked butter (p.11)
salt, freshly ground pepper

Making the basic stock
Slice the fish into large pieces. Heat the olive oil in a large pan and fry the
carrots, onion, shallots and leek for a few seconds. Add the tomatoes and the
tomato purée, arrange the fish on top, and then cover with the rest of the
flavourings. Continue to fry the contents of the pan for a minute or two, then
add 3 or 4 litres *(5¹/₄–7 pints)* of water. Season with salt and pepper.

Simmer for about 45 minutes, then sieve everything through the fine grill of a
mouli-légumes. Return the sauce to the pan and reduce, if necessary, until
you have obtained a good consistency.

Finishing the sauce
Add as much of the cream as you like, and then a little whisked butter to finish
the sauce and give it a velvety texture. Taste for seasoning.

Suggestions

This sauce is served with various fish or shellfish dishes (steamed, for example). It can be enriched by the addition of a little shellfish sauce with cream (p.17).

Left fairly plain, with either more or less cream, it can also be turned into a soup similar to Provençal fish soup.

White Wine Sauce with Cream

Sauce vin blanc à la crème

For four people

Preparation time – 45 minutes

50g *(2 oz)* butter
4 shallots, finely chopped
1 clove of garlic, crushed
1 glass *(100ml/4 fl. oz)* dry white wine or Sauternes
a slice of fresh ginger (optional)
1–2 teaspoons *beurre manié* (see note)
1 litre *(1¾ pints)* double cream or *crème fraîche* (p.23)
a pinch of curry powder or saffron
a squeeze of lemon juice
2–3 tablespoons whisked butter (p.11)
salt, freshly ground pepper

Melt the butter in a saucepan and throw in the shallots and garlic. Allow to simmer for a few moments, then add the white wine – either sweet or dry according to your taste.

Add the ginger, allow the liquid to reduce for 5 minutes, then add the *beurre manié* and stir it in. Stir in the cream, simmer to reduce and thicken a little, then season with salt and pepper. At the last moment, add a pinch of curry powder or saffron (whichever you prefer), a squeeze of lemon juice and, lastly, the whisked butter. Strain the sauce through a fine sieve, and it is ready for use.

Suggestions

This light cream sauce could be used with a fish dish or with chicken (a chicken breast steamed and served with a bouquet of little fresh vegetables, for example).

21

Note

Beurre manié is butter softened and worked with flour to a paste. It is used to give texture to sauces and to bind them. It can be added to an ordinary sauce, or to a stew such as a *civet*, when there is copious rich gravy that does not need reducing.

Rose Pink Sauce with Two Vinegars

Sauce rose légère au vinaigre

For four people

Preparation time – 30 minutes

2 tablespoons fresh tomato sauce (p.12)
1 tablespoon olive oil
red wine vinegar
sherry vinegar
1 small glass *(90ml/3 fl. oz)* dry white wine
3 tablespoons double cream or *crème fraîche* (p.23)
2–3 tablespoons whisked butter (p.11)
salt, freshly ground pepper

Put the tomatoes and olive oil in a small pan and whisk them together vigorously over a medium heat. Add a dash of each kind of vinegar and a small glass of white wine, and allow to reduce for a minute; then add the cream. Season with salt and pepper.

Whisk well with a wire whisk and finish the sauce by adding the whisked butter. Taste the sauce and add a little more vinegar or cream – whatever it needs; then simmer briefly.

Strain the sauce, which should be smooth, velvety and slightly pink in colour.

Suggestions

This light sauce should not be too strong; take care not to overdo the vinegar.

Use it with scallops or a plate of several kinds of fish served with a bouquet of different small vegetables, for example.

You could add chopped tarragon at the last minute; pour boiling water over the leaves before you chop them.

Crème Fraîche

Crème fraîche

Crème fraîche is simply double or whipping cream in which the natural lactic acids it contains are allowed to act until the cream has thickened considerably. It is usually then pasteurised. In most recipes, double cream may be used instead of *crème fraîche*; when there is a choice, this is indicated. If *crème fraîche* alone is given in the ingredients list, then it must be used, as its nutty taste and thick consistency are essential to the preparation involved. *Crème fraîche* can be found in some supermarkets but it tends to be very expensive, so it is worth making it yourself.

When making crème fraîche, use fresh pasteurised or unpasteurised, not ultra-pasteurised, cream. The chemical substances in ultra-pasteurised cream tend to slow down the thickening process and give the *crème fraîche* a slightly unpleasant metallic taste.

for 325ml (11 fl. oz) *crème fraîche*
300ml *(½ pint)* double cream
3 tablespoons buttermilk (active culture)

Place the cream and buttermilk in a saucepan, heat over a low heat until lukewarm to the touch, then remove from the heat and allow to stand in a warm place, covered, for 6–10 hours. Gently stir the cream to see if it is ready – if a thick layer has formed on top, but the cream is still liquid underneath, it is done (do not let it thicken too much or it will sour). Place the cream in a jar, stir to mix well, cover and place in the refrigerator overnight before using. The cream will finish thickening in the refrigerator and can be kept for up to a week before it starts to sour.

Aperitifs

Frédéric's Coquettes

Coquetier Frédéric

Take an egg-cup for each guest, and make enough of the following fillings to fill each one with successive layers of the three different purées.

1 A foie gras mousse or a chicken liver mousse (see poultry liver mousse with truffles, p.181). This mousse could be enhanced with a few drops of port and cognac, and a generous quantity of black pepper, freshly ground; the consistency should be on the thick side.

2 A fresh tomato sauce (p.12) with plenty of shallots, well reduced with a good pinch of finely chopped thyme leaves and flowers. Add extra cream and a dash of vinegar, and whisk in a dash of raw olive oil at the end. Taste for seasoning.

3 A mayonnaise of whole hard-boiled eggs shelled and chopped in a food processor, then mixed with some home-made mayonnaise to give a light and tender mixture. To avoid it becoming cloying, chop the eggs as briefly as possible. Season according to your own taste.

Finishing and serving the coquettes

You can use egg-cups or other pretty little individual dishes. Fill each one with successive layers of the fillings, using a pastry-bag or a teaspoon. Make the first layer of *foie gras*, the second of tomato and the third of egg mayonnaise. Chill in the refrigerator for an hour or two. Meanwhile, melt a little aspic, either bought or home-made.

Decorate the top of each coquette with sprigs of chervil, chopped truffles or caviare, or with little diamond-shaped pieces of tomato flesh. Cover the coquettes with a thin layer of aspic and return them to the refrigerator until you are ready to serve them.

Suggestions

Serve very cool, preferably with a stainless-steel spoon (not a silver one, because of the egg). Tell your guests to dig right to the bottom of the egg-cups to enjoy the mixture of colours and flavours all together.

Fresh Salmon Tartare in Smoked Salmon

Tartare de saumon frais en pannequet de saumon fumé

Take a nice piece of fresh salmon fillet and remove any bones with a pair of tweezers. Cut it into thin slices and then chop it with a large, sharp knife.

Put the chopped salmon into a bowl and add just enough mayonnaise to give it the texture of a steak tartare. Add a dash of lemon juice, a teaspoon of mustard, a little olive oil, a small quantity of gherkins, chopped, and a few snipped chive tips. Adjust the seasoning.

The tartare can now be rolled in little pieces of smoked salmon, as if they were stuffed pancakes. Serve on a dish decorated with sprigs of dill or a few chive tips.

This can be accompanied by a little mayonnaise, flavoured with a very fine purée of red peppers and some fresh tomato sauce (p.12), to which you can add a dash of vinegar to lighten the texture of the sauce.

Chicken Breasts in Tarragon Jelly

Blanc de poularde en gelée à l'estragon

You will need one or two large chickens, according to the number of guests. Remove the legs and thighs from each chicken, and reserve them to make a fricassee; or they can be roasted.

Put the whole chickens, minus the legs, into a large saucepan and cover them with a good home-made stock or consommé. Add leeks, celery, thyme, a bay leaf and a sprig of tarragon, bring to the boil and simmer for 15–20 minutes. Skim very thoroughly.

Take out the chickens and allow them to cool, then remove the white breast fillets very carefully with a sharp knife.

Clarify the consommé in which the chickens were cooked, if necessary, then add several leaves of gelatine, previously softened by soaking in cold water for 10 minutes. Add several sprigs of tarragon to the hot liquid and let it cool, then put it in the refrigerator until it is almost ready to set.

Cut the chicken breasts into little slices – each one just a mouthful, but not too thin. Put them on a cake rack and chill them in the refrigerator.

Decorate each slice of chicken breast with a leaf or two of tarragon and coat each one with the jelly. Give them several coats, and then chill again in the refrigerator until ready to serve.

Arrange the slices on a serving dish and hand round with cocktail sticks.

Suggestions
Instead of a jellied consommé you could use a *chaud-froid*, made with consommé and cream, to cover the pieces of chicken breast. Decorate with tarragon leaves after you have coated the pieces, and finish with a layer of clear jelly.

Fresh Figs and Melon with Parma Ham

Figues fraîches et melon au jambon de Parme

Choose some very ripe, perfect figs and small, heavily perfumed melons.

Cut the stalks off the figs and cut the fruits carefully into quarters. Peel them, then set them aside in a cool place.

Cut the melons in half and remove the seeds with a spoon, then cut the fruits into quarters and cut the flesh away from the skin with a flexible knife. Cut the flesh into bite-sized pieces.

Roll each piece of fig and melon in a little rectangle of very thinly sliced and carefully trimmed Parma ham. Serve with a cocktail stick stuck through each one.

Chicken Liver Mousse Canapés with Truffles and Pistachio Nuts

Canapé de mousse de foies blonds aux truffes et pistaches

Make the chicken liver mousse on p.182. Add a few pistachio nuts, skinned and cut into pieces.

Cut little round *croûtons* from a small French loaf (*ficelle*) and grill them to a golden brown in a moderate oven or grill; they should be an even golden colour.

Let the *croûtons* cool and cover them with the chicken liver mousse, either spreading it, or piping it on with a star-shaped nozzle. Decorate the top with truffles cut into thin julienne strips.

Suggestion
If the mousse seems too thick, lighten it with a little cream.

Little Skewers of Marinated Raw Salmon

Brochette de saumon sauvage mariné

Take a piece of filleted salmon, remove all the bones and slice it into small, even slices about as thick as a normal slice of ham. Keep in a cold place.

Shortly before you will be serving the appetisers, place the slices on a deep serving dish and soak them in a mixture of two-thirds olive oil to one-third fresh lemon juice for about 3 minutes.

When the colour of the salmon starts to lighten a little, drain the slices, put them on a clean dish and sprinkle them on both sides with chopped chervil and a few finely snipped chive tips. Then roll each one up like a cigarette and stick it with a cocktail stick.

Arrange the skewers on small dishes, decorating them attractively – perhaps with half a lemon peeled *à vif* and then finely sliced.

Note
To peel a lemon *à vif*, cut right through to the flesh so that you remove every shred of pith and all the inner skin that lies beneath the peel.

Little Snail and Mushroom Tarts

Croûstade d'une bouchée d'escargots forestière

Make a ragoût of snails with mushrooms (p.98); take care that it is well-flavoured with plenty of character, but not too liquid.

Make a classic *pâte brisée* (shortcrust pastry) and use it to make tiny tartlets no bigger than one mouthful, using the following ingredients:

150g *(5½ oz)* plain flour
90g *(3½ oz)* butter
a pinch of salt
1 tablespoon water

Fill each tartlet with a spoonful of the snail ragoût, and serve hot.

Scrambled Eggs with Tapenade

Œufs brouillés à la tapenade

Break some eggs into a salad bowl and beat them lightly with a fork, as if you were making an omelette, seasoning them with salt and pepper.

Scramble the eggs in the classic way in a heavy-bottomed pan over a gentle heat, adding a little fresh butter and stirring with a wooden spatula to prevent the eggs from sticking. Add half a tablespoon of water and finish the cooking over a very low heat, or in a bain-marie.

Incorporate more butter cut into pieces, or a little cream, towards the end of the cooking to obtain a very light, tender mixture. Taste for seasoning and serve in egg-cups or little individual dishes. Put a teaspoon of tapenade (see below) on the top.

To make the tapenade

Take 225g *(8 oz)* black olives and remove the stones. Add 50g *(2 oz)* of anchovy fillets, half a clove of garlic crushed to a paste, a few capers and some chopped fresh basil, together with 2 tablespoons of olive oil. Blend the mixture in a food processor for a few minutes to obtain a light, supple tapenade. Adjust the flavour according to taste, adding pepper if you want to. Keep in a covered glass jar in the refrigerator until needed.

Suggestions

Instead of tapenade, you could serve the scrambled eggs with a teaspoon of caviare or chopped truffles, or perhaps with some fresh tomato sauce (p.12).

31

Frogs' Legs Vinaigrette with Herbs

Vinaigrette de grenouilles aux herbes potagères

Choose medium-sized frogs' legs and cook them in butter in a large frying pan over a brisk heat. Season with salt and pepper, and add a little dry white wine. Cook, covered, without browning for about 10 minutes.

Drain the frogs' legs, keeping the cooking juices, and allow to cool. Bone the legs carefully and put them into a salad bowl.

Dress the boned legs with a little of the cooking liquid, a dash of good red wine vinegar and a little olive oil. Add some chopped fresh herbs – tarragon, chervil, basil, chives, etc.

Finish by adding little dice of fresh tomato and a finely chopped hard-boiled egg.

Taste for seasoning and bring the vinaigrette to the right balance of flavours by adding more or less of the various ingredients.

Serve just warm, in little individual dishes, decorated simply with a few chives.

New Potatoes
Stuffed with Braised Calf's Head

Petite pomme de terre nouvelle farcie à la tête de veau braisée

Buy the smallest new potatoes and peel them into the shape of little barrels, cutting one side flat so that they sit firmly on the plate. Hollow out the middles with a melon-baller.

Brown the potatoes lightly in butter in a large frying pan, season with salt and just cover them with water, or better still with consommé. Cover with a sheet of aluminium foil and cook over a moderate heat for 10 minutes or until just tender. Reserve them, covered, while you make the stuffing.

To make the stuffing, braise some pieces of boned calf's head with herbs, vegetables and spices (see the flavourings for the reduction in Beaujolais sauce, p.18), white wine, a little port and a seasoning of salt and pepper. Allow about 1½ hours' cooking time.

Fifteen minutes before the end of the cooking, add a little rice to thicken the sauce. When the stuffing is ready, chop it well in a food processor. Add a tablespoon of cream, together with a teaspoon of mustard and a little fresh tomato sauce (p.12). Adjust the seasoning and use a teaspoon to stuff the little potatoes with this mixture.

Decorate each one with a blanched lardon of streaky bacon, and heat briefly in the oven. Brown the tops lightly under the grill before serving.

Little Cocottes of Mussels with Chanterelles and Saffron

Cassolette de moules au safran et aux girolles naines

If possible, choose the small shiny mussels called *moules de bouchot*. Clean them carefully and remove their beards.

Melt a nut of butter in a large pan over a brisk heat, and add some chopped shallots. Moisten with dry white wine and throw in the mussels. Cover the pan and stir the mussels round from time to time with a wooden spatula. Allow 5 minutes' cooking time from the moment the liquid comes to the boil. The mussels are done when their shells have opened. Remove them with a slotted spoon and shell them. Keep them hot in a covered dish.

Trim some small chanterelles and cook them in a frying pan with a little butter. Meanwhile, make a classic *beurre blanc* (p.11) using some of the mussel cooking liquid, well filtered, to moisten it.

Add a pinch of saffron to the sauce to give it a good aroma, and season it carefully. Divide the mussels and chanterelles between several little individual cocottes or soufflé dishes and coat lightly with the sauce. Sprinkle with finely snipped chives and chopped chervil. Serve very hot.

Little Pastries with Snails in Green Butter

Petit feuilleté d'escargots au vert

Cook little bite-sized vol-au-vent cases made from home-made or frozen puff pastry.

Make a snail butter by mixing softened butter with fresh chopped herbs (use parsley, sorrel, chervil, young nettletops, spinach, etc.). Add a little garlic and some very finely chopped almonds, and season with salt and pepper and a squeeze of lemon juice.

Just before serving, put a little of this snail butter into each vol-au-vent case and put a snail, heated in its own cooking liquid and drained, on top.

Put a little more of the snail butter on top and heat through briefly in a moderate oven just before serving.

Spring

Country Salad with Œuf Mollet

Salade pastorale à l'œuf mollet

For four people

500g *(1 lb 2 oz)* raw young spinach or mixed young salad leaves
2 fillets of marinated herring
4 eggs
100g *(3¹/₂ oz)* butter
4 slices of day-old bread
a classic vinaigrette made with half groundnut oil/half olive oil, red wine
    vinegar, mustard, salt and pepper

Clean and pick over the salad leaves or spinach very carefully. Cut the herring fillets into thin strips and boil the eggs for exactly 6 minutes.

Cut the slices of bread into twenty little *croûtons* and fry them in the butter.

Just before serving the salad, toss the salad leaves or spinach in the vinaigrette and divide between four plates. Decorate the salad with strips of herring and place a shelled, soft-boiled egg in the centre, surrounded by *croûtons*.

Suggestions

Instead of spinach or small salad leaves, you could use tender young dandelion leaves.

You could add some blanched and sautéed lardons of streaky bacon at the last moment, either with the marinated herring fillets or instead of them.

Beef Carpaccio with Parmesan

Emincé de bœuf au parmesan

For six people

600g *(1 lb 5 oz)* fillet or sirloin of beef
6 tablespoons olive oil
juice of a lemon
a dash of red wine vinegar
freshly grated Parmesan
salt, freshly ground pepper

Cutting the beef

Chill the meat in the coldest part of the refrigerator or leave it for an hour in the freezer. Then cut it into twenty-four of the finest possible slices (they must be transparently thin).

Place the lightly salted slices between two oiled sheets of greaseproof paper or aluminium foil and flatten them with a rolling pin.

Seasoning and chilling the beef

Divide the slices between six plates and sprinkle them with olive oil, lemon juice, a few drops of vinegar and some freshly ground pepper. Add a scattering of freshly grated Parmesan if you like.

Leave to marinate in the refrigerator for 30 minutes before serving.

Suggestions

This dish could be served with a cold pasta salad in a light cream and mustard dressing, with chopped fresh basil and diced grilled peppers. Alternatively, it could be served with a green salad with a few finely sliced raw mushrooms sprinkled with lemon juice.

Freshwater Crayfish Salad with Asparagus Tips

Salade de queues d'écrevisses aux pointes d'asperges

For four people

2kg *(4½ lb)* best-quality asparagus
3kg *(6½ lb)* large freshwater crayfish
275ml *(9 fl. oz)* mayonnaise, freshly made
1 tablespoon Dijon mustard
1 lemon
1 tablespoon double cream
1–2 tablespoons dry white wine or white wine *court-bouillon* (p.14)
1 teaspoon each chives, tarragon and chervil, finely chopped
1 large tomato, peeled, deseeded and diced
a few green salad leaves
1 stick of celery, finely sliced
salt, freshly ground pepper

Cooking the asparagus

Choose good, fresh, green asparagus. Wash and trim them and tie them into bundles. Cook them in plenty of boiling salted water for 15–20 minutes, according to their size; do not overcook them or they will lose their flavour. Refresh them in cold running water and put them to drain on a rack or a clean cloth. Leave to cool, but do not refrigerate. When cool, cut the tips off and reserve.

Preparing the crayfish

Wash the crayfish and cook them in a large pan of strongly salted and peppered boiling water. Allow 2 minutes from the time the water returns to the boil. Then remove the pan from the heat and allow the crayfish to cool in their cooking liquid.

Preparing the mayonnaise

Flavour the mayonnaise with mustard, lemon juice, cream and a little white wine or white wine *court-bouillon*, adding more cream if necessary to obtain the right consistency. It should coat the back of a spoon lightly without sticking to it. Taste for seasoning.

Shelling and dressing the crayfish

Shell the crayfish tails, removing the black intestine. Place them in a bowl and coat them lightly with the mayonnaise, adding the freshly chopped herbs and small dice of fresh tomato.

Finishing and serving the salad

Cut half the salad leaves into ribbons, keeping the best ones whole. Arrange the whole leaves round the edges of four plates, as if you were making a nest. Put the ribbons of salad and the finely sliced celery in the centre.

Fill the nest with the crayfish in their dressing, mounding them up into little domes.

Stick the asparagus tips, cut in half lengthwise, into the crayfish so that they are sticking out like a hedgehog's spikes.

Suggestions

You can, if you like, add to the appearance of this salad by decorating it with sprigs of chervil, more diced tomato, or black truffles cut into fine julienne strips.

To make sure the salad is at its freshest, dress it at the last minute. It is best to prepare the ingredients shortly before you serve the salad, rather than making them beforehand and keeping them in the refrigerator.

Salad of Lambs' Trotters with Rémoulade Sauce

Saladier de pieds d'agneau rémoulade

For four people

8 lambs' trotters, cut in half lengthwise

for cooking the trotters

1 onion, stuck with a clove
1 carrot
1 *bouquet garni*
100ml *(4 fl. oz)* wine vinegar
1 tablespoon flour

for the mayonnaise

3 egg yolks
200ml *(7 fl. oz)* oil of arachide
2 tablespoons mustard
2 tablespoons double cream or *crème fraîche* (p.23)
50ml *(2 fl. oz)* lukewarm water (if necessary)
1½ teaspoons Worcester sauce
2 tablespoons capers
2 tablespoons raw onion, finely chopped
3 gherkins, finely chopped
2 tablespoons herbs (chervil, parsley and chives), finely chopped

for the garnish

flat parsley
chervil
whites of 2 hard-boiled eggs, chopped
salt, freshly ground pepper

Cooking the trotters

Scrape and flame the trotters and soak in cold water for an hour. Place the trotters in a large pan of water with the vegetables, *bouquet garni* and vinegar. Stir in a tablespoon of flour, season well and cook gently until the meat comes away from the bones. Bone the trotters and cut the meat into dice.

Making the mayonnaise

Make a mustardy mayonnaise in the usual way, using the quantities specified, and stir in the Worcester sauce, capers, onion, gherkins and herbs.

Dressing and serving the salad

Mix the lambs' trotters with the mayonnaise in a salad bowl, making sure they are well coated with the dressing. Sprinkle with the herbs for the garnish cut into little strips, and with the chopped egg white.

Suggestions

Make sure the mayonnaise is a good consistency and well flavoured. Make it while the trotters are still hot and serve it warm.

You could serve the trotters unboned, as this part of the operation is very lengthy and fiddly.

Iced Lobster
with a Tomato and Red Pepper Sauce

Soupe glacée de homard à la crème de tomates et poivrons doux

For four people

1 lobster, weighing 700–800g *(1²/₃–1³/₄ lb)*
1 large red pepper
2 tomatoes, skinned and deseeded
olive oil
a dash of red wine vinegar
6 tablespoons aromatic white wine *court-bouillon* (p.14)
6 tablespoons double cream
a pinch of saffron
a few sprigs of chervil
salt, freshly ground pepper

Cooking the lobster

Cook the lobster for 12–15 minutes in boiling salted water. Remove it from the pan, refresh it under cold water, and shell the tail and claws. Reserve in the refrigerator.

Preparing the vegetables and making the sauce

Grill the pepper until the skin is blackened and can be removed easily.

Cut the pepper and tomatoes into small pieces and purée them in a food processor. Add a little olive oil, a dash of vinegar, salt, freshly ground pepper and a little aromatic *court-bouillon*. Add the cream and finish the sauce with a pinch of saffron. Season well and strain it through a fine sieve. Chill.

Finishing and serving the soup

Take four soup plates and pour some of the tomato and pepper cream into each. Divide the lobster tail, cut into round slices, and the claws between the four plates and sprinkle with sprigs of chervil.

41

Gourmet's Layered Terrine of Foie Gras, Broad Beans and Artichoke Hearts

Mille-feuille gourmand en terrine

For eight people

1 litre *(1¾ pints)* port-flavoured jelly
8 large spinach leaves
2kg *(4½ lb)* tomatoes, peeled, deseeded and diced
2 shallots, chopped
1 tablespoon olive oil
1 *bouquet garni*
1 clove of garlic, peeled
2 chicken breasts
3 litres *(5¼ pints)* clarified chicken stock (optional)
6 tablespoons double cream or *crème fraîche* (p.23)
2 large or 3 small avocado pears
3 leaves of gelatine
400g *(14 oz)* fresh *foie gras*, cut into 1cm *(⅓ in)* slices
400g *(14 oz)* small, shelled broad beans, cooked and skinned
2 truffles, sliced
3–4 artichoke hearts, cooked and cut into sticks
salt

Preliminary preparations

Prepare the jelly, lightly flavoured with port. Let it cool until it is ready to set but still just liquid, then pour some into a well-chilled terrine, 25 × 10cm (10 × 4 in), and swill it round to cover the entire inside surface. Spoon more jelly down the sides to make sure you have a good layer of jelly. Keep in the refrigerator.

Wash the spinach leaves and blanch them for 30 seconds in boiling, salted water. Drain, refresh and spread out on a teatowel to drain.

Sweat the shallots in the olive oil for a minute or two, then add the tomatoes, *bouquet garni* and the clove of garlic. Reduce over a moderate heat, stirring occasionally, until you have a thick purée. Season generously with salt and pepper.

Poach the chicken breasts, preferably still attached to the carcass, in chicken stock (or boiling salted water flavoured with herbs and vegetables) for 20 minutes (see p.28). Remove them, allow to cool and then cut the breasts into large thin slices with a sharp knife.

Peel the avocados and remove the stones. Heat the cream in a small pan and dissolve the gelatine, previously soaked in cold water for 10 minutes and drained, in the hot cream. Cut the avocados into large pieces and add them to the cream. Season with salt and pepper and blend to a purée in a food processor.

Making the terrine

Use half the spinach leaves to line the bottom of the terrine with its coating of jelly. Arrange a layer of slices of *foie gras* on top. Cover this layer with cold jelly and place in the refrigerator to set.

Next, put in a layer of half the avocado cream and put the broad beans on top, pushing them into the mousse with a fork. Use a spoon to cover this with another layer of jelly. Allow to set in the refrigerator, then put in a layer of half the sliced chicken and cover this with the tomato purée.

Arrange the remaining slices of chicken on top, again coat the top with jelly, scatter on the sliced truffles and chill once more.

Next, put in a layer of the remaining avocado mousse and the artichoke hearts. Chill again.

Lastly, put in a layer of the remaining *foie gras* and finish with the last of the spinach leaves, arranging them neatly to give the terrine a well-finished appearance.

Coat once more with jelly and chill in the refrigerator for 24 hours before serving.

Suggestions

This recipe is rather fiddly and complicated to make. To serve the terrine, unmould it by dipping it briefly into hot water, then cut it into thin slices with a sharp flexible knife, also dipped into hot water.

In this terrine, the combination of flavours and colours should be well balanced; make sure that each element is as well flavoured as it can be.

You could use fresh peas or French beans instead of broad beans in the first avocado layer, and accompany the terrine with a little vinaigrette flavoured with diced tomato and chopped fresh herbs.

Sautéed Chicken Livers with Green Peppercorns and a Purée of Parsley

Petit sauté de foies blonds au poivre vert et à la purée de persil

For four people

12 large pale chicken livers from free-range chickens
300g *(10½ oz)* potatoes, peeled and cut into pieces
1 leek, washed, white part only
1kg *(2¼ lb)* parsley, washed
200ml *(7 fl. oz)* double cream or *crème fraîche* (p.23)
100g *(3½ oz)* butter
a dash of brandy
2 tablespoons meat glaze
green peppercorns
salt, freshly ground pepper

Preliminary preparations

Clean the chicken livers, removing threads and green parts. Open them up and flatten them somewhat with the blade of a large, heavy knife; keep them in a cool place.

Cook the potatoes and leek in boiling, salted water for about 15 minutes, then add the parsley and cook for a further 15 minutes.

Drain the vegetables and parsley and transfer them to a food processor. Reduce them to a purée, adding enough cream to give a fairly liquid consistency. Season the purée and keep it hot in the top of a bain-marie.

Cooking the chicken livers

Take a little of the butter and heat half of it in each of two large frying pans. Fry the chicken livers over a brisk heat so that they brown but do not cook right through or become dry; they should be a nice pink inside, but not bloody. Remove them from the pan and keep them hot without cooking any further.

Pour the butter out of the pans and deglaze each one with a dash of brandy and a tablespoon of water. Combine the juices in one pan, then add the meat glaze and green peppercorns and whisk in the remaining butter, a little at a time, over a gentle heat.

Serving the chicken livers

Pour some of the parsley purée on to four plates, place the chicken livers round the edge and coat each one lightly with the green peppercorn sauce. Serve at once.

Suggestions

The success of this dish depends on the quality of the chicken livers, which can be rather bitter. The parsley purée should be freshly made, not reheated, or it will lose its fresh taste and beautiful green colour.

Skate Vinaigrette in a Bed of Greenery

Aile de raie sur lit de verdure

For four people

4 pieces of skate, each weighing 200g *(7 oz)*
1 litre *(1¾ pints)* aromatic white wine *court-bouillon* (p.14)
200g *(7 oz)* mixed salad leaves (chicory, endive, lamb's lettuce, batavian endive, etc.)
200g *(7 oz)* fresh young spinach
50g *(2 oz)* butter
a pinch of grated nutmeg
1 clove of garlic, peeled

for the vinaigrette
4 tablespoons olive oil
3–4 tablespoons groundnut oil
1 tablespoon sherry vinegar
1 tablespoon red wine vinegar
1 teaspoon mustard
1 tablespoon chopped chervil and snipped chives
salt, freshly ground pepper

Poach the skate by bringing it to the boil in a wide pan containing the *court-bouillon* and a little water. As soon as it starts to bubble, turn down the heat and cook gently for 10 minutes. Meanwhile make the vinaigrette.

Lift out the pieces of skate, and remove the skin from both sides.

Heat the salad leaves and spinach very gently in the butter for 4 minutes, with a pinch of nutmeg and a whole clove of garlic.

Divide the hot salad between four plates, place the pieces of skate on top, dress with the vinaigrette and sprinkle with the chopped herbs. If necessary, warm the salads very gently in a moderate oven with the door open. Serve hot.

Suggestion

You could add a skinned, deseeded and diced tomato to the vinaigrette to give it a little colour.

Little Goujons of Whiting with Herb Butter

Goujonnettes de merlan au beurre printanier

For four people

4 very large fresh whiting fillets (see suggestions)
1 carrot, cut into little pieces like confetti
500ml *(16 fl.oz)* whisked butter (p.11)
1 tablespoon chives, finely snipped
1 tablespoon tarragon, finely chopped
1 lemon
salt, freshly ground pepper

Preliminary preparations

Skin the whiting fillets and cut them into *goujons* (cut across slightly on the bias, giving pieces the size of a slender potato chip). Place them side by side and well spaced out on a buttered baking sheet.

Heat the oven to its highest setting.

Cook the little pieces of carrot by bringing them to the boil in a pan of salted water. Drain them as soon as the water comes to the boil.

Add lemon juice to the whisked butter, taste it for seasoning and add the freshly chopped herbs. Keep warm.

Cooking the whiting

Just before serving, sprinkle the fish lightly with a little water and put it in the very hot oven. The cooking will be practically instantaneous. Remove the fillets from the oven at once and divide them between four hot plates, lifting them carefully with a metal spatula.

Coat the fillets lightly with the whisked butter sauce with its herbs, then scatter the little lozenges of carrot over the top. Serve at once.

Suggestions

This light, cheap and simple dish is an excellent way of enjoying the particularly pleasant flavour of whiting, a common fish but not devoid of interest. However, you could equally well cook other kinds of fish this way. If you want to succeed, take great care over the cooking time, which varies according to the type of fish: whiting is light and delicate, John Dory or turbot are dense and firm, and take longer to cook. Hake or coley would also be good substitutes and would cook quickly like whiting.

Gratin of Dublin Bay Prawns with Spinach

Gratin de langoustines aux épinards

For four people

24 large Dublin Bay prawns
250ml *(8 fl. oz)* shellfish sauce with cream (see p.17)
1kg *(2¼ lb)* spinach
80g *(3 oz)* butter
1 clove of garlic
a pinch of grated nutmeg
2 tablespoons double cream or *crème fraîche* (p.23), whipped
half a lemon
salt, freshly ground pepper

Preliminary preparations

Shell the Dublin Bay prawns, wash them well and remove the black intestines by making a slight incision in each one. Use the shells, heads and claws to make a shellfish sauce.

Prepare the spinach by plunging it into boiling salted water for a minute, then refreshing it in cold water, draining it and pressing it to extract all the excess water. Let it cook gently in a little of the butter with a clove of garlic and a pinch of nutmeg. When it is tender, season it, divide it between four small individual *gratin* dishes, and keep it hot. Pre-heat the grill.

Cooking the Dublin Bay prawns

Heat the remaining butter in a non-stick frying pan and cook the shelled Dublin Bay prawn tails quite briskly until they change colour and whiten. Add a ladle of the shellfish sauce and let it simmer for a moment before removing from the heat. Add 2 tablespoons of whipped cream and a little lemon juice.

Finishing and serving the *gratins*

Divide the Dublin Bay prawns between the four *gratin* dishes and coat them with the shellfish sauce, then place them close to the hot grill (or use a salamander) to glaze the tops to a delicate amber colour. Serve at once.

Suggestions

Avoid stirring the sauce from the time you have added the whipped cream, which is there to give the glaze a beautiful golden colour.

If you prefer, you can replace the spinach with an interesting purée, such as parsley (p.44).

To make a really well-flavoured sauce, use some additional lobster or freshwater crayfish shells, reserved in the freezer from a former dish where they were not required.

Large Freshwater Crayfish Grilled with Garlic Butter

Grosses écrevisses 'pattes rouges' grillées au beurre d'ail

For four people

6 large freshwater crayfish per person – about 1.5kg (*3 lb 2 oz*)
6 tablespoons olive oil

for the garlic butter
100g (*3¹/₂ oz*) softened butter
1 clove of garlic, finely crushed
1 shallot, finely chopped
2 tablespoons finely chopped herbs (tarragon, chives and parsley)

Preparing the crayfish
Pre-heat the oven to Reg. 4/350°F/180°C.

Wash the crayfish in cold water and remove the black intestines by breaking and removing the central fin – this can be done only with live crayfish. Cut them in half lengthwise as if they were lobsters. First take a small paring knife and plunge it right through the head shells. Keep them shell-side up and season well with salt and pepper. Make the garlic butter.

Cooking and serving the shellfish
Heat the olive oil in a large pan and place the shellfish in it, flesh-side down, to sear them. After a few seconds, when they have started to brown lightly, turn them over and finish cooking them in the oven for 3–4 minutes, basting the tops with the garlic butter.

Serve at once on large heated plates. Give everyone a small oyster or snail fork to eat them with.

Suggestions
This recipe must be made at the very last moment. Choose very large crayfish (see introduction, p.2). The dish can be served either as a first course or as an appetiser with drinks.

48

Minute Steak of Wild Salmon with Aigrelette Sauce

Minute de saumon sauvage sauce aigrelette

For four people

800g *(1¾ lb)* wild Scotch salmon fillet
2 teaspoons butter, softened
500ml *(16 fl. oz) sauce aigrelette* (p.15)
salt, freshly ground pepper

Preliminary preparations

Ask your fishmonger to cut the boned salmon fillet into very thin, large escalopes, no thicker than a slice of ham – or, alternatively, do it yourself. Reserve in the refrigerator.

Prepare the *sauce aigrelette* and keep it warm.

Brush four large plates with butter and season them lightly with salt and pepper. Pre-heat the oven to Reg. 2/300°F/150°C.

Cooking and serving the salmon

Arrange the slices of salmon to cover the bottom of each plate, touching but not overlapping. Just before serving, put the plates in the oven for 2–3 minutes.

As it cooks, the salmon will become paler. Avoid overcooking it; it is best to take it out of the oven while the slices are still red in the middle, as the heat of the plates will continue to cook it.

Coat the salmon lightly with *sauce aigrelette,* well flavoured with fresh herbs.

Suggestions

This dish can be served either as a first course or as a light main course. Salmon cut as thin as this can be cooked only on individual plates. You can test it by pressing it with your finger to see if it is done; it cooks practically as soon as it goes into the oven.

Warm Salad of Frogs' Legs and Freshwater Crayfish

Vinaigrette tiède de grenouilles et de queues d'écrevisses aux
herbes

For four people

2kg *(4½ lb)* freshwater crayfish
15–20 pairs of frogs' legs
150g *(5½ oz)* butter
50ml *(2 fl. oz)* dry white wine
a dash of olive oil
juice of half a lemon
a dash of white wine vinegar
a dash of soya sauce (optional)
1 tomato, peeled, deseeded and finely diced
1 hard-boiled egg, finely chopped
chives and tarragon, finely chopped
salt, freshly ground pepper

Cooking the crayfish

Wash the crayfish and drop them into a large pan of water seasoned generously with salt and pepper. Allow to cook for 2–3 minutes after the water comes back to the boil, then remove them from the liquid and let them cool. Shell them, removing the black intestines.

Cooking the frogs' legs

Melt a generous quantity of butter in a large frying pan and cook the frogs' legs for 5–6 minutes without browning. Season with salt and pepper, add the white wine and cook for a further 5 minutes, then allow to cool in their own liquid. Bone the legs carefully, keeping them in their original shape as far as possible.

Finishing and serving the salad

Put the crayfish tails and boned frogs' legs in a stainless steel pan over a gentle heat. Add 2–3 tablespoons of the strained cooking juices from the frogs' legs. Add the olive oil, a squeeze of lemon juice, a little wine vinegar and, lastly, a dash of soya sauce. Let all the different ingredients blend together, taste the sauce for seasoning, then add the diced tomato and chopped hard-boiled egg. Sprinkle with chopped tarragon and chives and serve at once in little individual dishes or small bowls.

Eggs in a Sorrel Nest

Œufs au nid d'oseille

For four people

8 generous handfuls of tender young sorrel
75g *(2½ oz)* butter
6 tablespoons clarified stock or veal demi-glace
300ml *(½ pint)* double cream or *crème fraîche* (p.23)
8 eggs
4 tablespoons meat glaze or the juices from a roast joint
   (preferably veal)
a pinch of icing sugar
salt, freshly ground pepper

Cooking the sorrel

Wash the sorrel carefully and blanch it in a large pan of boiling, salted water. When the water comes back to the boil, allow a few seconds, then drain and refresh the sorrel and drain it again thoroughly.

Melt 50g *(2 oz)* butter in a frying pan and stir in the sorrel, seasoning it with salt, pepper and a pinch of icing sugar. Allow to simmer gently and add the stock. Reduce it somewhat, then add the cream. Leave to simmer gently.

Cooking and serving the eggs

Fry the eggs gently in the remaining butter and finish them off by placing them under a hot grill for a minute. Do not overcook them.

Make a nest of sorrel on each of four plates, and slide two eggs into the middle of each one. Pour a thread of hot meat juices around each one and serve at once.

Suggestions

You could equally well poach the eggs in unsalted water acidulated with vinegar. Serve with little *croûtons* fried in butter and rubbed with garlic.

Paul Blanc's Freshwater Fish Medley

L'assiette du val de Saône 'Paul Blanc'

For four people

650g *(1 lb 7¹/₂ oz)* pike
650g *(1 lb 7¹/₂ oz)* perch
650g *(1 lb 7¹/₂ oz)* sander
400g *(14 oz)* freshwater crayfish

for the nage

2 carrots, channelled and sliced (see note)
2 white spring onions, cut into julienne strips
the white part of 2 leeks, cut into julienne strips
1 stick of celery, cut into julienne strips
1 stick of fennel, cut into julienne strips
a sprig of basil, cut into strips
juice of a lemon
half a bottle of Pouilly-Fuissé

100g *(3¹/₂ oz)* fresh green peas
100g *(3¹/₂ oz)* small French beans, cut diagonally into short lengths
1 tablespoon thick double cream or *crème fraîche* (p.23)
300g *(11¹/₂ oz)* butter, cut into dice
a few sprigs of chervil
chopped parsley
salt, freshly ground pepper

Preliminary preparations

Clean the pike, perch and sander, and fillet them, removing all the bones. Cut them into pieces weighing about 50g *(2 oz)*.

Making the *nage* and cooking the crayfish

Put all the ingredients for the *nage* into a pan with 1 litre *(1³/₄ pints)* of water. Season, bring to the boil and simmer for 12–15 minutes.

Wash the crayfish and throw them into the simmering *nage*. Let them cook for 5 minutes, then remove and shell them. Keep the vegetables and shelled crayfish tails hot.

Cooking the fish and vegetables

Heat the oven to Reg. 5/375°F/190°C. Place the pieces of fish in a buttered oven dish, season them and moisten them with the strained *nage*. Cook them briefly, without boiling, until they are firm. Remove and keep hot.

Cook the peas and the French beans separately in boiling, salted water until just done and still slightly crisp. Drain and keep hot.

Making the sauce and serving the fish

Reduce the cooking liquid from the fish by three-quarters and add the cream. Then gradually whisk in the butter, a little at a time, without boiling, as if you were making a *beurre blanc.* Taste for seasoning and keep warm. On four heated plates, arrange pieces of each different fish, the vegetables from the *nage,* peas, beans and crayfish tails. Coat lightly with the *beurre blanc,* then sprinkle with chopped parsley and chervil.

Note

Paul Blanc was George Blanc's uncle, one of the great master-chefs just after the war.

To prepare the carrots for this recipe, use a canelle knife to cut thin scores or channels down each carrot. This gives the slices, when cut, a pretty, flower-like appearance.

Smoked Salmon Pancakes with Caviare

Crêpes parmentier au saumon fumé et au caviare

For four people

for the pancakes
200g *(7 oz)* butter, clarified
250g *(8 ½ oz)* potatoes, peeled
2 tablespoons milk
1½ tablespoons plain flour
1½ eggs
2 egg whites
1½ tablespoons double cream
salt

150g *(5 ½ oz)* smoked salmon, thinly sliced
150ml *(¼ pint)* whipping cream
50g *(2 oz)* caviare (optional)
1 tablespoon chives, finely snipped
juice of half a lemon
salt, freshly ground pepper

Preliminary preparations

Prepare the clarified butter and the pancake batter according to the instructions on p.215, using the measurements given here.

Cut the smoked salmon into pieces the size of a very small pancake (about the size of a slice of a large tomato).

Mix the cream with the chives, lemon juice and freshly ground pepper.

Cooking and serving the pancakes

Heat a large, reliable steel omelette pan or crêpe pan and put in a tablespoon or two of the clarified butter. Start to fry several pancakes, using three-quarters of a small ladle of batter for each one. They will become round and rise a little. Now, before turning the pancakes, place a slice of smoked salmon on each one, so that it is more or less coated in the batter. Turn the pancakes with a metal spatula and then remove them from the pan. Drain them briefly on paper towels, then serve at once in soup plates with the cream and the caviare.

Suggestions

Cook the pancakes fairly briskly – but take care not to overcook them, as pancake and salmon must both be very tender. Do not add salt to the cream, as the smoked salmon is already quite salty.

Monkfish with Saffron, Asparagus and Morels

Lotte au safran, aux pointes d'asperges at aux morilles noires

For four people

700g *(1²⁄₃ lb)* monkfish fillets, trimmed by the fishmonger
1kg *(2¹⁄₄ lb)* asparagus
150g *(5¹⁄₂ oz)* fresh morels (preferably black morels)
300g *(10¹⁄₂ oz)* butter
2 shallots, chopped
4 tablespoons white wine
250ml *(8 fl. oz)* double cream or *crème fraîche* (p.23)
a pinch of saffron
a few sprigs of chervil
salt, freshly ground pepper

Preliminary preparations

Cut the monkfish into little round slices about the thickness of a thin steak. Butter a large *gratin* dish or roasting tin and spread out the pieces of monkfish side by side. Reserve in a cool place or cover with a damp cloth.

Trim the asparagus, keeping only 2–3 inches of the tips, and cook these in boiling water until just tender: allow about 7–8 minutes and test by piercing with a knife. Drain, refresh under cold water and keep on one side.

Meanwhile, wash the morels in several changes of cold water, remove the stalks and sweat them in a little of the butter along with the chopped shallots in a covered pan. Cook for 8–10 minutes, then drain in a wire sieve and set on one side. Reserve the juices.

Pre-heat the oven to its hottest setting.

Making the sauce

Strain the cooking juices from the mushrooms into a small saucepan, add the white wine and allow to reduce by half. Add the cream and reduce by half again, then add the remaining butter, cut into dice, whisking to emulsify the sauce and give it a light texture. Add the saffron and season with salt and pepper.

Add the mushrooms to the sauce and add a little more cream if necessary. Taste again for seasoning and keep hot.

Cooking and serving the monkfish

Just before serving, sprinkle the monkfish with a little water and slide them into the hot oven. Heat the asparagus while the fish cooks; it will need little more than 1 minute. Test the fish by pressing with your finger, then transfer to a serving dish. Coat lightly with the morel sauce and arrange the asparagus tips decoratively in little bouquets round the outside. Add a few little sprigs of chervil to emphasise the delicacy and subtlety of the dish.

Suggestions

You could make this dish using shellfish, such as Dublin Bay prawns or slices of lobster, and serve it in diamond-shaped pastries, lightly coated with the sauce.

Medley of Lobster
and Freshwater Crayfish with Caviare

Panaché de homard et d'écrevisses au caviar

For four people

1 litre *(1¾ pints)* aromatic white wine *court-bouillon* (p.14)
1 lobster, weighing 800g *(1¾ lb)*
20 freshwater crayfish *(about 1kg/2¼ lb)*
5 tablespoons classic *beurre blanc* (p.11)
80g *(3 oz)* butter
50g *(2 oz)* caviare
3 tablespoons double cream
salt, freshly ground pepper

Preliminary preparations

Let the *court-bouillon* simmer for 30 minutes, then add the lobster and let it cook gently for 10 minutes. Remove it, pierce the front of the head with a sharp knife and let it drain, head downwards.

Add the crayfish to the *court-bouillon*, simmer for 2–3 minutes and then allow to cool in their cooking liquid. Shell the lobster tail and claws and cut the tail into twelve equal slices.

Drain and shell the crayfish carefully, removing the black intestines. Reserve.

Making the sauce

Melt a little butter in a medium sauté pan, and cook the lobster and crayfish briefly over a brisk heat. Add a little of the *court-bouillon* and all the cream. Simmer for 1 minute without boiling – the shellfish should be hot right through, but if they are allowed to boil it will spoil the texture.

To finish and serve the dish

Arrange the lobster and crayfish in individual dishes, sharing them out equally. Keep them warm while you heat the sauce. Add the *beurre blanc* a spoonful at a time, and at the very last moment stir in the caviare. Taste the sauce for seasoning (it should be very light) and pour it over and round the shellfish. Serve at once.

Suggestions

This rather costly recipe can be either a rich first course or a main dish. Avoid adding any salt during the cooking, and season the sauce only after you have added the caviare. Do not heat it further once the caviare is in.

If you like, you can replace the cream in this recipe with the following preparation. Cut up the heads of the shellfish and sauté them in butter with 2 chopped shallots. Flame with 1–2 tablespoons of brandy and then add 250ml *(8 fl. oz)* double cream and allow to reduce for 15 minutes. Strain through a fine sieve.

Gratin of Tripe
with White Wine and Herbs

Tripes gratinées au vin blanc et aux aromates

For four people

1.5kg *(3½ lb)* prepared tripe
200g *(7 oz)* butter
2 large onions, finely sliced
2 shallots, finely chopped
a sprig of thyme
1 bay leaf
1 litre *(1¾ pints)* dry white wine
1 litre *(1¾ pints)* clarified chicken stock or water
4 carrots, finely sliced
1 tablespoon tarragon, finely chopped
1 tablespoon chervil, finely chopped
dried breadcrumbs (home-made)
salt, freshly ground pepper, *quatre épices* (see note)

Cooking the tripe

Buy ready-cooked tripe and cut it into little strips 5mm *(¼ in)* wide. Melt 150g *(5½ oz)* of the butter in a large enamelled iron casserole and cook the onions and shallots. When they have turned a pale golden colour, add the tripe together with the thyme and bay leaf.

Add the white wine and stock or water, season with salt and pepper and a little *quatre épices*, and simmer, covered, for 1½ hours. If the liquid evaporates too much, add a little more water.

Add the carrots and cook for a further 1½ hours, then taste for seasoning and stir in the fresh herbs.

Finishing and serving the tripe

Transfer the tripe to a large *gratin* dish and sprinkle the top with bread-crumbs. Dot with the remaining butter and brown in a hot oven.

Suggestions

This dish can be prepared in advance and reheated; it will be all the better for it.

Note

Quatre épices is a blend of spices generally used in charcuterie. It consists of: 4 parts ground black pepper, 1 part powdered cloves, 1 part powdered ginger, 1 part grated nutmeg.

Shin of Veal with New Vegetables

Jarret de veau aux légumes printaniers

For six people

1.5kg *(3½ lb)* shin of veal in one piece
30g *(1 oz)* butter
2 tablespoons oil of arachide
500ml *(¾ pint)* good home-made stock or water
1 bouquet garni
450g *(1 lb)* peas in their pods, shelled
450g *(1 lb)* new carrots, diced
450g *(1 lb)* new potatoes, diced
225g *(½ lb)* new silver onions
1 marrow bone
300ml *(½ pint)* double cream or *crème fraîche* (p.23)
juice of half a lemon
1 tablespoon each of chopped parsley and sage or chives
salt, freshly ground pepper

Cooking the veal

Melt the butter and oil in a heavy pan and brown the shin on all sides. Season it with salt and pepper, then add the *bouquet garni* and the stock or water. Allow to simmer for 1½ hours.

Now add all the little vegetables and let them cook gently for 10 minutes; then add the marrow bone, seasoned with salt on its cut ends, and cook for 10 minutes more.

Serving the veal

Transfer the veal to a board, slice it finely and arrange the slices on a heated serving dish.

Arrange the vegetables all round it in little groups. Slice the marrow and arrange on top. Keep hot.

Pour the cream into the pan and let it reduce and thicken. Taste the sauce for seasoning, strain it and add a squeeze of lemon juice. Sprinkle the sauce over the vegetables and scatter the chopped fresh herbs over the top.

Suggestion

You might prefer to cook the vegetables separately, so that they each have their correct cooking time.

Escalopes of Brill
with Tomato and Mustard Seeds

Escalope de barbue à la graine de moutarde et à la tomate

For four people

1 brill or turbot, weighing about 2kg *(4¹/₂ lb)*, filleted
a little butter
250ml *(8 fl. oz)* tomato sauce (p.13)
a pinch of thyme flowers, finely chopped
150ml *(¹/₄ pint)* plus 1 tablespoon double cream or *crème fraîche*
(p.23)
3 teaspoons coarse Meaux mustard
juice of half a lemon
salt, freshly ground pepper

Preparing the escalopes

Make a horizontal incision in each fillet so that you can open it up like a book; it should make an escalope about the thickness of an escalope of veal. Place each escalope between two sheets of aluminium foil and flatten it with a cutlet bat or heavy knife; this breaks up the sinews in the fish, so that the escalope does not shrink when it is cooked.

Butter a roasting tin or other ovenproof dish (or possibly two) and spread out the escalopes side by side. Heat the grill.

59

Making the sauce

Heat the tomato sauce, let it reduce a little, then adjust the seasoning and add the chopped thyme flowers. Stir in a tablespoon of cream and keep hot.

Cooking the brill

Whisk the remaining cream energetically and add the mustard. Season with salt and pepper and a dash of lemon juice. Spread the surface of the brill escalopes with the mixture, using the back of a spoon.

Place the escalopes under the grill to glaze and cook at one and the same time. Lift the escalopes to see if they are cooked – it should take no more than 2–3 minutes; the escalopes should glaze to a beautiful amber colour.

Serving the brill

Put a layer of the tomato sauce over the bottom of four large heated plates and lay the escalopes on top. Serve at once.

Suggestions

Serve either as a first course or as the main part of the menu.

The cooking of these escalopes is a delicate operation; they should be done at the precise moment that the whipped cream is perfectly glazed to a golden colour. If the heat is too high and the glaze is ready before the fish is cooked, place the cooking dish over a gentle heat for a few moments.

Braised Beef with Calves' Feet and Carrots (my mother's recipe)

Aiguillette de bœuf braisée aux carottes et aux pieds de veau
(recette de ma mère)

For four to six people

1kg *(2¼ lb)* braising beef, taken from the blade or thick flank (the most gelatinous cuts)
2 calves' feet, split in half
200g *(7 oz)* butter
10–12 small onions
1kg *(2¼ lb)* carrots
salt, freshly ground pepper

Cooking the beef

Pre-heat the oven to Reg. 2/300°F/150°C.

Heat 50g *(2 oz)* of the butter in a large cast-iron casserole and brown the piece of beef on all sides over a brisk heat, seasoning it with salt and pepper as it cooks.

Add a few tablespoons of water to dissolve the caramelised meat juices on the bottom of the pan. Arrange the calves' feet round the piece of beef, cover the casserole and cook for 1½–2 hours in the low oven. From time to time, check that there is enough moisture in the pan, adding a few more tablespoons of water if necessary. Add the onions halfway through the cooking.

Preparing the carrots

Keep the carrots whole if they are new, and cut them into even strips if they are old.

Melt a little butter in a small saucepan and put in the carrots. Let them cook gently for a few minutes, then just cover them with a little water and season them with salt and pepper. Cook for 10 minutes (less if they are new carrots). Drain the carrots and finish cooking them by putting them in with the beef for the last 20 minutes of the cooking time.

Serving the beef

Cover a heated serving dish with a layer of carrots and arrange the beef, cut into even slices, and the boned calves' feet on top.

Finish the sauce by whisking in the butter, cut into small cubes, without allowing it to boil. It should be a beautiful golden colour.

Suggestion

This dish can be kept hot for some time, or even reheated if necessary.

Note

When I first joined the family business, my mother used to conjure up this comforting, countrified dish, using her sure instinct and excellent judgement; it was the toast of all the guests in the restaurant.

Aiguillettes of Duck with Beaujolais Sauce

Aiguillettes de canard beaujolaise

For four people

2 large ducks, each weighing about 2kg *(4½ lb)*
100g *(3½ oz)* butter
750ml *(27 fl. oz)* Beaujolais sauce (p.18)
1 carrot, sliced
1 onion, sliced
a sprig of thyme
half a bay leaf
200g *(7 oz)* wild mushrooms in season (ceps, chanterelles,
    morels, etc.)
60g *(2 oz)* small silver onions
a dash of vinegar   ⎫
1 shallot, chopped ⎬ optional
a pinch of sugar   ⎭
salt, freshly ground pepper

Cooking the ducks

Pre-heat the oven to Reg. 8/450°F/230°C.

Melt a little of the butter in a large enamelled iron casserole and put in the trussed ducks and their giblets – necks, wingtips, etc. Add the carrot, onion and herbs. Season well and roast in the hot oven for 15–20 minutes.

Take out the ducks, remove the legs, cutting through the ball-and-socket joints under the body, and return the legs to the oven for 8–10 minutes to finish cooking.

Remove the duck breasts from the carcasses with a sharp knife and keep them warm. They should still be rather pink.

Making the sauce and the garnish

Spoon all the fat from the duck cooking juices. Chop up the carcasses and return them to the casserole with the juices.

Add the Beaujolais sauce and let it reduce slowly, so that the flavours intensify. Meanwhile, glaze the small onions.

Clean the mushrooms, slice them if necessary, and blanch them in boiling salted water for 5–10 minutes. Drain well, then sauté them briskly in half the remaining butter. Drain and keep hot.

Finishing the sauce and serving the duck

Taste the sauce for seasoning, reduce if necessary, adding a shallot and a dash of vinegar if you think it needs them. Strain through a fine sieve and whisk in the remaining butter cut into small pieces.

Just before serving, slice the duck breasts into small slices and divide them between four heated plates. Place a lightly browned leg beside them and garnish with the mushrooms and small onions. Coat lightly with the Beaujolais sauce.

Suggestions

Large ducks, though less tender than ducklings, have more flavour. Make sure the duck breasts are not overdone. When making the sauce, give it plenty of character, but it should not be too sharp. If you wish to improve on the presentation of this dish, you could add one or two of Mère Blanc's pancakes (p.215) or a little mousse of courgettes. You could also cut the skin of the ducks into thin strips and fry them in butter before laying them over the top of the sliced breast fillets.

Fish with Sauerkraut

Choucroute de poisson

For four people

1 haddock fillet, weighing 500g *(1 lb 2 oz)*
500ml *(16 fl. oz)* milk
1 monkfish tail, weighing 500g *(1 lb 2 oz)*, cut into 8 pieces
1 salmon fillet, weighing 500g *(1 lb 2 oz)*, cut into 4 pieces
2 red mullet, weighing about 250g *(8½ oz)* each
4 scallops, shelled
3–4 handfuls of seaweed or 500ml *(16 fl. oz)* aromatic white wine
    court-bouillon (p.14)
1kg *(2¼ lb)* cooked sauerkraut
150ml *(¼ pint)* dry white wine
500ml *(16 fl. oz)* classic *beurre blanc* (p.11)
salt, freshly ground pepper

63

Cooking the fish

Poach the haddock, cut into four pieces, in simmering salted milk for 10 minutes. Place the rest of the fish on a bed of seaweed in the steamer of a large *couscoussier*. Half-fill the bottom with boiling water, cover the steamer, place it on its base and steam for 5–8 minutes. Check that the fish are cooked, and keep warm. If you haven't any seaweed, put aromatic white wine *court-bouillon* in the base instead of water.

Heating the sauerkraut and *beurre blanc*

Meanwhile, heat the sauerkraut in the white wine until it is hot right through. Heat the *beurre blanc* gently and keep it warm.

Serving the fish

Spread out the sauerkraut on a large heated serving dish and arrange the pieces of fish on top, having first lifted the fillets from the red mullet and discarded the bones.

Serve, with the warm *beurre blanc* in a sauceboat.

Suggestions

You can vary the fish and shellfish according to the occasion (Dublin Bay prawns and fine fish such as turbot and bass for a celebration; cod and hake for a simpler meal). You can also add a few steamed potatoes.

Marine Fricassee with Sauternes and Curry

Panaché de la mer au sauternes et au curry

For four people

1kg *(2¼ lb)* various kinds of fish and scallops (choose from bass, brill, turbot, monkfish, red mullet, salmon, etc.)
750ml *(27 fl. oz)* white wine sauce with cream (p.21), but made with Sauternes or other sweet wine
curry powder
a little butter
salt, freshly ground pepper

to decorate

1 carrot, cut into little pieces like confetti
sprigs of fresh chervil

Preparing the fish

Cut all the fish into even pieces about the size of your little finger (*goujonettes*). Cut the scallops in half horizontally.

Butter a large baking sheet generously and arrange all the pieces of fish and scallops side by side. Pre-heat the oven to its highest setting.

Finishing the sauce

Make the Sauternes sauce and season it well with a good pinch of curry powder.

Cooking and serving the fish

Shortly before serving, season the fish with salt and pepper and sprinkle with water sparingly. Cook rapidly in the oven for 3 minutes or so. The evaporation of the water will prevent the fish from drying out. Test for doneness by pressing with your finger.

When they are just cooked through, transfer the pieces of fish to four heated soup plates, coat lightly with the sauce and decorate with carrot confetti and sprigs of chervil.

Suggestions

In spring you could add asparagus tips to this dish, and possibly Dublin Bay prawns cooked separately; cook them gently in butter in a covered pan.

Tournedos Steaks with Morels and Cream

Tournedos aux morilles à la crème

For four people

4 tournedos steaks, weighing 200g *(7 oz)* each, taken from the
   prime end of a beef fillet
250g *(8¹/₂ oz)* fresh morels or 100g *(3¹/₂ oz)* dried morels
2 shallots, finely chopped
150g *(5¹/₂ oz)* butter
1 teaspoon Dijon mustard
250ml *(8 fl. oz)* thick double cream
100ml *(4 fl. oz)* port
100ml *(4 fl. oz)* meat glaze
1 tablespoon truffle juice
salt, freshly ground pepper

Preparing the morels

Wash the mushrooms carefully, removing the stalks, and slit them down one side so that you can wash out every trace of sand. If you are using dried mushrooms, put them to soak the day before, in 2–3 times their own volume of water. When they are clean, stew the morels in a little water in a covered pan for 15 minutes and drain them.

Heat 50g *(2 oz)* of the butter and soften the chopped shallot gently, then add the mushrooms and the mustard followed by the cream. Let it reduce to intensify the flavour of the morels and become velvety and lightly thickened. Season lightly; morels do not need much pepper.

Cooking the steaks

Fry the steaks in 50g *(2 oz)* of the butter, making sure the outsides are nicely browned but have not yet developed a thick crust. Use a spoon to turn them, to avoid piercing them while they cook. When they are perfectly done, transfer them to a heated serving dish and keep warm.

Making the sauce and serving the steaks

Deglaze the pan with the port, dissolving all the caramelised juices. Add the meat glaze, reduce a little and then add the truffle juice.

Season carefully. Away from the heat, whisk in the remaining butter, cut into pieces, to give the sauce a nice consistency and a good gloss.

Serve the steaks on hot plates with the morels in their sauce round them and the strained port sauce over the top.

Suggestions

This dish seems simple, but you do have to know how to fry meat, and balance the sauce – a delicate business. It must both look and taste good – a matter of using the different ingredients harmoniously, which can be accomplished only with practice.

Braised Calf's Head with Little Vegetables

Braisé de tête de veau aux petits légumes

For four people

half a calf's head, boned

for the stock

2 onions
4 shallots
1 stick of celery
2 carrots
1 whole head of garlic
2 tomatoes
half a bay leaf
a sprig of thyme
2 cloves

150g *(5½ oz)* butter
2 tablespoons oil of arachide
100ml *(4 fl. oz)* madeira
100ml *(4 fl. oz)* Noilly Prat or other dry white vermouth
300ml *(½ pint)* dry white wine
1 litre *(1¾ pints)* good veal or chicken stock (or consommé)
300g *(10½ oz)* small carrots and turnips, cut into the shape of cloves of garlic
100g *(3½ oz)* small silver onions
100g *(3½ oz)* button mushrooms or wild mushrooms
a nut of *beurre manié*
a pinch of sugar
salt, freshly ground pepper

Cooking the calf's head

Blanch the calf's head for 3 minutes in boiling, salted water, then drain, refresh under cold water, drain again and reserve. Soften the vegetables and herbs for the stock in 50g *(2 oz)* of the butter for several minutes, stirring them round with a wooden spoon.

Trim the calf's head, removing all the rough parts round the tongue. Skin the tongue and cut away any fatty bits.

Cut the head into large even pieces as you would when making a stew. Heat a little oil and butter in a large frying pan and brown the pieces lightly, then remove with a slotted spoon. Drain well and put them into the pan with the vegetables and herbs.

Deglaze the pan with the madeira and vermouth and flame it. Add the white wine, reduce a little to get rid of the acidity in the wine, then add the stock or consommé. Simmer for about 1½ hours.

Finishing and serving the calf's head

Shortly before you serve the dish, cook the little shaped vegetables and the mushrooms in boiling salted water. Put the onions in a small sauté pan with enough water just to cover them, and add a large nut of butter. Season with salt and a pinch of sugar, and cook, covered, until the water has evaporated and the onions are lightly glazed.

Remove the pieces of calf's head and put them into a heated serving dish. (Use a large deep dish or a handsome rustic braising pan.) Arrange the little vegetables over and around the pieces of calf's head.

Add a nut of *beurre manié* to the sauce, adjusting the texture and seasoning. Whisk in 50g *(2 oz)* of the butter in small pieces, strain the sauce through a wire sieve over the calf's head and vegetables, and serve very hot.

Suggestions

This dish can be prepared in advance and reheated gently without spoiling the flavour.

Rich Blanquette
of Shellfish with Wild Mushrooms

Blanquette de homard, langouste, langoustines et écrevisses aux
   champignons noirs

For four people

1 lobster, weighing 600g *(1 lb 5 oz)*
1 crawfish, weighing 700g *(1²/₃ lb)*
12 Dublin Bay prawns
12 freshwater crayfish
1 litre *(1³/₄ pints)* aromatic white wine *court-bouillon* (p.14)
250ml *(8 fl. oz)* shellfish sauce (p.17), made with the shells of the
   shellfish used in this recipe
100g *(3¹/₂ oz)* butter
175g *(6¹/₂ oz)* morels or false morels *(Helvella lacunosa)*
3—4 tablespoons double cream or *crème fraîche* (p.23)
3 tablespoons whisked butter (p.11)
a pinch of saffron
1 teaspoon tarragon, chopped
1 teaspoon chives, snipped
a few sprigs of chervil
salt, freshly ground pepper

Preparing the shellfish

Wash the shellfish thoroughly. Plunge the lobster and crawfish into plenty of boiling, well-salted water and cook for 15 minutes, then drain well. Boil the freshwater crayfish in the aromatic white wine *court-bouillon* for 1 minute, then take them off the heat and let them cool in their cooking liquid.

Shell the crawfish tail and the lobster claws and tail. Cut the tails into rounds. Shell the crayfish and remove the black intestine.

Make the shellfish sauce using all the shellfish shells and heads.

Cooking the mushrooms

Stew the well-washed mushrooms in a little of the butter until they are tender.

Finishing and serving the *blanquette*

Shell the raw Dublin Bay prawns and let them firm up in butter in a large sauté pan over a brisk heat for 1 minute.

Add the mushrooms and crayfish tails and moisten with 3 tablespoons of the aromatic crayfish *court-bouillon* and enough shellfish sauce just to cover them. Bring to the boil and simmer gently for an instant; stir in the cream to lighten the sauce if necessary. Add the lobster claws and sliced lobster and crawfish tails and stir in a little whisked butter. Heat, without boiling, and taste for seasoning; add the saffron, tarragon and chives at the last moment.

Serve in deep, heated soup plates or individual dishes, giving some of each shellfish to each person. Scatter a few sprigs of chervil over the top and serve at once.

Suggestions

This rich dish could be simplified by reducing the number of different shellfish used. You could also use different mushrooms, such as chanterelles or St George's mushrooms.

Fricassee of Chicken with Garlic and Foie Gras

Fricassée de poularde de Bresse aux gousses d'ail et au foie gras

For four people

1 large free-range chicken, weighing 2kg *(4¹/₂ lb)*, cut into 8 pieces

for cooking the chicken

2 carrots, sliced
2 onions, sliced
2 cloves of garlic, unpeeled
2 shallots, peeled
bouquet garni of thyme, bay leaf and a clove

120g *(4¹/₂ oz)* butter
125ml *(¹/₄ pint)* dry white wine or consommé
12 cloves of garlic, unpeeled
1 small glass of water
4 tablespoons thick double cream
100g *(3¹/₂ oz) foie gras* mousse or chicken liver mousse (p.182)
a dash of white wine vinegar (optional)
salt, freshly ground pepper

Cooking the chicken

Pre-heat the oven to its highest setting. Melt the butter in a large enamelled iron casserole. Put in the pieces of chicken, all the trimmings and bones, and the vegetables and herbs.

Stir them round, season with salt and pepper, and cook, covered, in the hot oven. After 15 minutes, add the white wine or consommé, or a mixture of both. Add the 12 cloves of garlic and cook for a further 15–20 minutes or until the chicken is done. Test by piercing the thighs with a sharp knife – a colourless bead of moisture means it is done; if the juices are still rosy, give it a little longer.

Finishing and serving the fricassee

Transfer the pieces of chicken to a heated serving dish and keep them hot. Remove the cloves of garlic from the sauce and peel them. They should be cooked through; if they are not, cook them in the sauce for a little longer, adding more liquid if necessary. Keep them hot with the chicken.

Skim the sauce, add a small glass of water and the cream, reduce gently, then strain through a wire sieve into a small pan.

Add the *foie gras* or chicken liver mousse and whisk until the sauce is just coming to the boil. Taste for seasoning and strain over the pieces of chicken. Serve at once with Mère Blanc's Vonnas pancakes (p.216), made without sugar, or with a fresh young vegetable.

Suggestions

Remove the chicken breasts from their bones after cooking and return the bones to the sauce before it is reduced, or use a very strong well-flavoured stock for the cooking.

Do not let the sauce boil energetically after adding the *foie gras* – it will spoil the texture. Add a little dash of vinegar at the last moment if you like.

Christiane's Chicken

Poulet de Bresse Christiane

For four people

1 large free-range chicken, weighing 2kg *(4½ lb)*, cut into 8 pieces
25g (1 oz) butter
1–2 tablespoons oil of arachide
2 white onions, sliced
2 cloves of garlic, crushed
4 tomatoes, skinned, deseeded and diced
1 *bouquet garni*
1 coconut
2 tablespoons double cream or *crème fraîche* (p.23)

for the rougail

2 tomatoes, skinned, deseeded and diced
2 spring onions, chopped (or chives)

for the achards

2 carrots cut into thin strips
150g *(5½ oz)* green cabbage, cut into thin strips
100g *(3½ oz)* French beans
olive oil
saffron, cayenne pepper and a pinch of curry powder

salt, freshly ground pepper

Cooking the chicken

Heat the butter and oil in a large iron casserole and brown the pieces of chicken all over, seasoning them as they cook. Add the onions, garlic, two of the diced tomatoes and the *bouquet garni*. Moisten with 250ml *(8 fl. oz)* water and simmer, covered, for about 45 minutes, turning the pieces over frequently.

Making the coconut milk

Pierce holes in the top of the coconut and drain off the milk, then break open the coconut and remove the flesh. Pulverise the flesh in a liquidiser, then put it in a bowl and moisten it with boiling water. Strain and press, catching the milk in a bowl. Repeat the process and add the two batches of coconut milk to the chicken, 5 minutes before the end of its cooking time, together with the cream.

Finishing and serving the chicken

Remove the pieces of chicken. Reduce the sauce if it seems too liquid and strain it through a fine wire sieve. Season it, add the two remaining diced tomatoes and pour the sauce over the chicken. Serve very hot with the following accompaniments and some plain, boiled rice.

Rougail

Season the diced tomatoes with salt and pepper and mix with the chopped spring onions or chives.

Achards

Sauté the vegetables in olive oil for 5 minutes, seasoning with salt, pepper, saffron, cayenne pepper and curry powder.

Author's note

I owe this recipe to Christiane Agnetti, who helped me to put together the recipes for this book.

Sweetbreads with Mushrooms, Young Broad Beans and Noilly Prat Sauce

Ris de veau aux champignons et aux fèves de printemps,
  sauce noilly

For four people

700g *(1²⁄₃ lb)* veal sweetbreads
1kg *(2¹⁄₄ lb)* young broad beans in their shells
200g *(7 oz)* cultivated mushrooms
1 tablespoon flour
100g *(3¹⁄₂ oz)* butter
2 shallots, chopped
4 tablespoons Noilly Prat or other dry white vermouth
100ml *(4 fl. oz)* dry white wine
200ml *(7 fl. oz)* double cream or *crème fraîche* (p.23)
salt, freshly ground pepper

Preliminary preparations

Prick the sweetbreads with a fork and soak them in a bowl of cold water placed under a trickling tap to eliminate all the blood.

Simmer in salted water for 3–4 minutes, then refresh in cold water, skin them and remove any discoloured parts and fat. Cut into generous slices and reserve on a plate.

Shell the broad beans, cook them in boiling salted water for 1 minute, then remove the skin from each bean. Reserve.

Wash the mushrooms, slice them and sauté them in 50g *(2 oz)* of the butter. Set them aside with their juice.

Cooking and serving the sweetbreads

Shortly before serving the sweetbreads, dip the slices in flour, tapping them to remove any excess, and fry them briefly in 50g *(2 oz)* of the butter until they are a pale golden colour. When they are done, arrange them on a heated serving dish and keep them hot while you prepare the sauce.

Soften the shallots in the same butter and deglaze the pan with the vermouth and white wine, stirring to dissolve all the caramelised juices in the pan. Reduce the liquid by half, then add the cream. Allow to reduce until the sauce is light and velvety. Strain it into a sauté pan.

Add the broad beans and mushrooms with some of their cooking liquid to the sauce. Taste for seasoning, pour lightly over the sweetbreads and serve very hot.

Suggestion

You could at different seasons vary the vegetables used for garnishing the sweetbreads, perhaps using chanterelles or morels, small fresh peas or asparagus tips.

White Cheesecake

Tarte au fromage blanc

For eight people

300g *(10½ oz)* shortcrust pastry
300g *(10½ oz) fromage blanc* or quark (40 per cent fat)
4 eggs, separated
50g *(2 oz)* icing sugar
100ml *(4 fl. oz)* thick double cream
grated zest of a lemon
icing sugar

Make your own favourite shortcrust pastry, and let it rest for an hour or two, then roll it out and use it to line a well-buttered tart ring. Pre-heat the oven to Reg. 6/400°F/200°C.

Whisk the *fromage blanc* in a bowl with the egg yolks, icing sugar, cream and lemon zest.

Whip the egg-whites to a very firm snow and fold them lightly into the cheese mixture. Use this mixture to fill the tart shell, and bake for 30 minutes.

Remove from the ring, transfer to a rack to cool and sprinkle with icing sugar before serving.

Grandmother's Orange Gâteau

Gâteau à l'orange grand-mère Blanc

For four people

2 medium oranges
150g *(5½ oz)* butter
150g *(5½ oz)* icing sugar
2 eggs
115g *(4 oz)* plain flour
1 teaspoon baking powder

for the icing
115g *(4 oz)* icing sugar
1 teaspoon or more Kirsch

Pre-heat the oven to Reg. 7/425°F/220°C.

Sieve the flour and baking powder. Pare the zest from the oranges, chop it finely and reserve it.

Soften the butter until creamy, and mix it with the icing sugar, beating with a wooden spoon until you have a soft, smooth mixture.

Add the strained juice of one orange, beat in first one egg and then the other, and stir in the sieved flour and baking powder. Beat with a wooden spoon until smooth, and add the orange zest, keeping back a spoonful to decorate the cake.

Butter and flour a straight sided flan tin or sandwich tin. Pour in the mixture and bake for 10 minutes, then lower the heat to Reg. 5/375°F/190°C and bake for a further 10 minutes.

Remove and cool on a rack. Mix the icing sugar with the juice of half an orange and a spoonful of Kirsch.

When the cake has cooled a little, ice it with the orange and Kirsch icing and sprinkle it with the reserved orange peel.

Suggestions
You could decorate the top of the cake with fresh berries or crystallised fruit. Serve it with chilled custard.

Chocolate Meringue Cake

Gâteau meringué au chocolat

For four people

for the meringue
4 egg whites
125g *(4¹/₂ oz)* caster sugar
125g *(4¹/₂ oz)* icing sugar

for the chocolate ganache
30g *(1 oz)* cocoa powder (unsweetened)
200ml *(7 fl. oz)* plus 4 tablespoons thick double cream
300g *(10¹/₂ oz) couverture* or cooking chocolate

Making the meringue

Pre-heat the oven to Reg. ¹/₄/225°F/110°C.

Whisk the egg whites by hand or with an electric beater until they are fairly firm, then beat in the caster sugar. Delicately fold in the icing sugar with a wooden spatula.

Using a large piping bag, pipe spirals of meringue on to a piece of greaseproof paper on a baking sheet to make two 20cm *(8 in)* discs. Bake for about 3 hours.

Making the chocolate *ganache*

Bring the 200ml *(7 fl. oz)* cream to the boil in a wide pan. Break the chocolate into little pieces. When the cream boils, remove it from the heat and throw in the chocolate, stirring until it has completely dissolved and you have a smooth mixture. Pour this chocolate *ganache* through a sieve into a bowl and leave to stiffen in the refrigerator for about 2 hours.

Beat the *ganache* energetically with a wooden spoon until it becomes slightly paler. Then add the 4 extra tablespoons of cream to finish it.

Serving the meringue cake

Put one of the meringue discs on a serving dish. Pipe all the chocolate *ganache* on top or spread it on with a spoon. Place the second meringue disc on top, sprinkle it with cocoa powder and keep the cake cool until ready to serve it.

Suggestions

For a different presentation, you could top the cake with a little extra whipped cream and sprinkle it with chocolate shavings, then with icing sugar.

Rhubarb Upside-down Tart

Tarte à l'envers à la rhubarbe

For eight people

750g *(1 lb 10 oz)* rhubarb
125g *(4½ oz)* moist brown sugar
125g *(4½ oz)* caster sugar
2 eggs
60ml *(2½ fl. oz)* double cream or *crème fraîche* (p.23)
20g *(¾ oz)* fine pastry flour
350g *(12 oz)* flaky pastry or shortcrust pastry

Wash and peel the rhubarb stalks, cut them in half lengthwise and then into pieces 5cm *(2 in)* long.

Put layers of the rhubarb in a tart tin or cake tin, and alternate the layers with sprinklings of brown sugar and caster sugar.

Beat the eggs in a bowl and mix them with the cream and the flour. Pour this batter over the rhubarb.

Pre-heat the oven to Reg. 8/450°F/240°C.

Roll out the pastry a little more than ½cm *(¼ in)* thick; allow enough to cover the sides of the mould as well as the top.

Make a round of the pastry to fit the top of the tart and with the trimmings make a strip ½cm *(¼ in)* wide; moisten it with water and stick it round the edge of the tin to give depth to the pastry base.

Make a hole in the centre to let out the steam, and bake for 50 minutes, lowering the heat after 10–15 minutes. Serve it turned out upside down like a *tarte tatin*.

Suggestions

Serve the tart cold with vanilla-flavoured custard.

You could cook the rhubarb first, before putting it into the tart tin (drain it well if there is too much liquid). It will then take less time to cook.

Cherry Clafoutis

Clafoutis aux cerises

500g *(1 lb 2 oz)* ripe cherries, stones removed (choose firm, meaty
 cherries)
4 eggs
180g *(6½ oz)* sugar
100g *(3½ oz)* plain flour, sieved
a pinch of salt
1–2 tablespoons Kirsch
250ml *(8 fl. oz)* milk
80g (3 oz) butter plus 15g *(½ oz)* for buttering the dish
icing sugar

Whisk the eggs in a bowl with the sugar, sieved flour, salt and Kirsch. When
the batter is completely smooth, gradually beat in the milk. Melt 40g *(1½ oz)*
of the butter and whisk it into the batter.

Pre-heat the oven to Reg. 4/350°F/180°C.

Butter a porcelain or glazed earthenware *gratin* dish. Put a layer of the batter
in the bottom, cover it with a layer of cherries and fill the dish to the top with
the batter. Sprinkle with the remaining butter cut into little pieces and cook
in the oven for 40 minutes.

Sprinkle the top with icing sugar as soon as it comes out of the oven.

Serve cold from its dish, using a cake server to cut it.

Passion Fruit Mousse

Mousse aux fruits de la passion

For four people (two per person)

10 passion fruits (preferably from Kenya, as these have the best
 flavour)
3 leaves of gelatine
300ml *(½ pint)* whipping cream
70g *(2½ oz)* caster sugar

Cut the passion fruits in half and scoop out the insides into a bowl. Purée the
fruit pulp in a food processor and strain it through a fine sieve.

Soften the leaves of gelatine in cold water for a few minutes, then melt them gently in a little hot water, without boiling. Mix with the passion fruit, whisking vigorously to prevent the gelatine from forming lumps. Chill, stirring from time to time.

Whip the cream with the sugar until it is fairly firm. Then add the whipped cream to the passion fruit juice and fold it in carefully until you have a smooth mixture.

Spoon the mixture into eight little 8cm *(3 in)* soufflé dishes or ramekins and chill for an hour or two before serving. Serve two to each person.

Suggestions

You could serve this mousse on a *génoise* sponge base. Dip it briefly into very hot water and turn it out on to a plate.

Accompany the mousse with fresh soft fruit and a fresh fruit sauce, such as raspberry or strawberry.

Nut Meringues from Mâcon

Succès mâconnais

For four people

for the nut meringues
6 egg whites
125g *(4¹/₂ oz)* caster sugar
60g *(2 oz)* icing sugar
60g *(2 oz)* ground almonds, sieved
60g *(2 oz)* ground hazelnuts, sieved

for the praline
50g *(2 oz)* blanched almonds
50g *(2 oz)* icing sugar
half a vanilla pod

for the praline cream
6 egg yolks
250g *(8½ oz)* caster sugar
100g *(3½ oz)* plain flour
1 vanilla pod
500ml *(16 fl. oz)* milk
200ml *(7 fl. oz)* whipping cream
100g *(3½ oz)* praline (see below)
a pinch of salt

Making the nut meringues

Pre-heat the oven to Reg. ¼/225°F/110°C.

Whisk the egg whites by hand or with an electric beater, adding the caster sugar when they have formed a fairly firm snow. Beat in the caster sugar thoroughly and then fold in the icing sugar carefully with a wooden spatula, followed by the almonds and hazelnuts.

Use a pastry bag to pipe the meringue into round discs about 5cm *(2 in)* across on a sheet of greaseproof paper on a baking sheet. Cook them in the very low oven for about 3 hours.

Making the praline

Toast the almonds. Melt the sugar in a little water (in a copper pan, if possible) and boil until it turns a pale amber colour.

Add the toasted almonds, stir them round and pour them out on to a piece of marble or an oiled baking sheet. Allow them to cool and then crush them with a pestle and mortar. The praline is now ready to use.

Making the praline cream

Heat the milk with the split vanilla pod. Beat the caster sugar and egg yolks together in a large bowl. Add the flour and a pinch of salt. When the milk comes to the boil, pour it on to the egg mixture in a stream, whisking all the time. Return to the saucepan and place over a moderate heat, stirring until the mixture comes to the boil.

Strain and allow to cool. Whip the cream. Add the praline and the whipped cream to the custard.

Serving the nut meringues

Put half the nut meringues on to a serving dish and pipe on a layer of the praline cream or spread it on with a spoon.

Put the remaining meringues on top, shiny side up, and sprinkle with icing sugar. Keep chilled until you are ready to serve them.

Suggestions

These individual nut meringues could also be served as one large one by making two large meringue discs of the same size. Fill and decorate in the same way and serve chilled.

Bitter Chocolate Marquise

Marquise au chocolat amer

For eight people

250g *(8¹/₂ oz)* unsweetened chocolate
250g *(8¹/₂ oz)* softened butter
250ml *(8 fl. oz)* vanilla pastry cream
5 egg yolks
1 teaspoon strong coffee

Melt the chocolate in a saucepan over a gentle heat, or in the top half of a double boiler. Pour it into a bowl and mix in the butter, pastry cream, egg yolks and coffee. Whisk vigorously with a balloon whisk for 20 minutes.

When the mixture is smooth and light, spoon it into little oiled individual moulds or soufflé dishes and chill. Unmould just before serving.

Suggestions

This is delicious served with a coffee sauce. You could, if you liked, decorate the marquises with rosettes of piped whipped cream.

Summer

Preserved Ducks' Giblets in a Salad

Salade aux gésiers confits

For four people

200g *(7 oz)* mixed salad leaves
8 preserved ducks' gizzards
2 tablespoons chopped herbs (chives, tarragon and parsley)
100ml *(4 fl. oz)* vinaigrette (see p.45), but use 1 tablespoon
    walnut oil instead of the olive oil, and wine vinegar only

Dress the well-washed and dried salad leaves with the vinaigrette flavoured with walnut oil and arrange them prettily on four plates, alternating the different colours.

Heat the gizzards gently in a frying pan to melt the fat that surrounds them. Cut them into thin slices and place them on top of the salads.

Sprinkle with freshly chopped herbs and serve warm.

Suggestions

This salad is very simple and can be embellished. For example, you could add fresh walnuts and fine julienne strips of orange zest, or better still a julienne of fresh black truffles. You can use goose or chicken gizzards instead of duck.

Marinated Tuna Fish with Limes and Olive Oil

Emincé de thon frais mariné au citron, à l'huile d'olive et à la fleur
    de thym

For four people

600g *(1 lb 5 oz)* raw tuna fish fillet (preferably pink in colour)
3 limes
olive oil
1 tablespoon chives, snipped
1 tablespoon each tarragon and chervil, chopped
a pinch of finely chopped thyme
4 tablespoons double cream or *crème fraîche* (p.23)
1 teaspoon coarse Meaux mustard
a dash of red wine vinegar
salt, freshly ground pepper

Preparing the tuna fish

Slice the tuna into large thin slices about as thick as a slice of ordinary ham.

Make a marinade using two-thirds lime juice to one-third olive oil; this is easily done if you put the squeezed lime juice into a measuring jug. Season with salt and pepper and stir in the herbs.

Soak the slices of tuna in the marinade until they start to change colour – about 2–3 minutes. Then drain and spread out on four large serving plates.

Making the mustard sauce and serving the tuna fish

Whisk the cream in a bowl with salt and pepper, add a teaspoon of mustard and a dash of red wine vinegar.

Serve the fish with the sauce on the side.

Suggestions

This first course is easy to prepare and can equally well be made with raw salmon or other oily fish.

Crawfish Mayonnaise with Small Seasonal Salads

Salade variée à la langouste bretonne

For four people

1 crawfish, weighing 800g–1kg *(1¾–2¼ lb)*
600g–1kg *(1 lb 5 oz–2¼ lb)* varied salad leaves (any wild or
   cultivated small salad leaves, lettuce thinnings, etc.)
2 large firm red tomatoes, skinned and seeded
sprigs of tarragon, chives and chervil
100ml *(4 fl. oz)* vinaigrette (p.45)
250ml *(8 fl. oz)* mayonnaise
salt, freshly ground pepper

Preliminary preparations

Cook the crawfish for 15 minutes in a large pan of rapidly boiling salted water. Refresh it under cold water, make an incision between its antennae and leave it upside down in a colander to drain.

Wash and pick over the different salad leaves and dry them well in a cloth.

Dressing and serving the crawfish

Shell the tail and claws of the crawfish, and cut the meat into large even pieces. Stir it into the mayonnaise and carefully mix in the herbs. If the mayonnaise seems too thick, add a little vinegar, a little water into which you have squeezed half a lemon, or some aromatic white wine *court-bouillon* (p.14).

Toss the salad leaves in the vinaigrette. Divide the dressed crawfish between four large plates. Cut the tomatoes into quarters and then cut the quarters in half again. Arrange tomatoes and salad leaves prettily around the crawfish and decorate with herbs – chive tips and sprigs of tarragon and chervil.

Suggestions

You can vary the salad that surrounds the crawfish by adding cooked French beans, fresh garden peas or mangetout peas – whatever you like that is in season at the time. I sometimes add a teaspoon of tarragon-flavoured mustard to the mayonnaise.

Freshwater Crayfish in a Meursault Court-bouillon

Court-bouillon d'écrevisses au meursault

For four people

1kg *(2¼ lb)* freshwater crayfish
2 bottles of Meursault or other dry white wine

flavourings for the court-bouillon

a sprig of fresh thyme
2 cloves of garlic
half a bay leaf
1 lemon, peeled *à vif* and sliced
1 onion, stuck with a clove
2 shallots
3 young carrots, sliced
25 black peppercorns, coarsely crushed
50g *(2 oz)* coarse sea salt

Preparing the *court-bouillon*

Pour the wine into a large stainless-steel pan. Add 500ml *(¾ pint)* water and all the flavourings for the *court-bouillon*. Bring to the boil and simmer for about 30 minutes. Allow to cool; strain and reheat when you are ready to cook the crayfish.

Cooking the crayfish

Just before cooking, draw out the black intestines from the crayfish by breaking and removing the central tail fin.

When the *court-bouillon* comes to the boil, throw in all the crayfish at once. Bring the *court-bouillon* back to simmering point and then allow the crayfish to cook for 3 minutes.

Remove the crayfish with a skimmer or slotted spoon and arrange them in a large bowl or fruit dish. Cover them with the strained *court-bouillon*, which you have tasted for seasoning, and serve hot, cold or even lukewarm. Eat the crayfish with your fingers.

Suggestions

Serve as a first course with the same wine as you used for the *court-bouillon*. If you keep the crayfish in their cooking liquid overnight, they will develop even more flavour. Rough country bread and good butter make the best accompaniment.

Fresh Tuna Fish Tartare with Caviare

Tartare de thon blanc frais au caviar

For four people

800g *(1¾ lb)* raw white tuna fish, trimmed
3 shallots, very finely chopped
100g *(3½ oz)* capers, chopped
2 gherkins, finely chopped
4 tablespoons olive oil
2 limes (one peeled *à vif*)
3 tablespoons continental parsley, chopped
3 tablespoons chives, snipped (keep the tips for garnish)
a dash of Tabasco
a small (or large) pot of caviare or salmon eggs
salt, freshly ground pepper

Cut the carefully trimmed tuna fish into slices and then chop to the texture of steak tartare.

88

*Frédéric's Coquettes
and Fresh Salmon Tartare
in Smoked Salmon.*

(pp. 27 and 28)

Gourmet's Layered Terrine of Foie Gras,
Broad Beans and Artichoke Hearts.

(p.42)

*Freshwater Crayfish Salad
with Asparagus Tips.*
(p.38)

*Braised Beef
with Calves' Feet and Carrots.*

(p.60)

*Braised Calf's Head
with Little Vegetables.*
(p.67)

*Little Goujons of Whiting
with Herb Butter.*

(p.46)

Marinated Chicken Alexandre.
(p.93)

Chicken Breasts 'Club des Cent'.
(p.106)

Mix the fish in a bowl with the shallots, capers, gherkins, olive oil, the juice of one lime, half the herbs, the Tabasco and seasoning. Taste the mixture and add more of any of these to your taste.

With wetted spoons mould the tartare into four quenelle shapes. Place one on each of four plates. Sprinkle them with chopped parsley and caviare or salmon eggs, and decorate with the chive tips and quarters of the peeled lime.

Suggestions

Instead of tuna fish, you could equally well use salmon or a firm white fish such as bass or striped bass. The caviare, instead of being sprinkled on top, can be mixed into the tartare with the other ingredients.

To perfect this dish, you can serve it rolled in thin slices of smoked salmon and decorate it with fresh herbs – chive tips and dill for example.

Salpicon of Lobster with Truffles

Salpicon de homard à la brunoise de légumes

For four people

1 lobster, weighing 1.2kg *(2 lb 10 oz)* altogether
a stick of celery
3 carrots
1 leek
50g *(2 oz)* fresh black truffles (or preserved truffles)
250ml *(8 fl. oz)* mayonnaise made with three parts oil of arachide
    to one part olive oil
6 tablespoons aromatic white wine *court-bouillon* (p.14), or juice
    of half a lemon
salt, freshly ground pepper

Preliminary preparations

Bring a large pan of salted water to the boil and cook the lobster for about 15–20 minutes. Remove and drain.

Cut the vegetables into very fine dice to make the *brunoise*. Cook them in boiling salted water for 5 minutes, refresh and drain them, then set them aside in a bowl.

Shell the tail and claws of the lobster and cut it into large dice (*salpicon*). Reserve.

Cut half the truffles into dice the same size as the vegetables, and the other half into fine julienne strips.

Making the vegetable *brunoise*

Mix the diced truffle with the vegetables and stir them into the mayonnaise, which should be well flavoured and rather on the liquid side – add some white wine *court-bouillon* or lemon juice, and some truffle juice if it is available, to obtain the right consistency. Transfer this *brunoise* to four small soufflé dishes or soup plates.

Serving the lobster

Divide the *salpicon* of lobster between the four plates and scatter the truffle julienne on top, to set off the whiteness of the lobster.

Suggestions

This rather extravagant dish makes a refreshing first course for a party. It can also be made with crawfish and the vegetables can be varied with the seasons to include fresh green peas, French beans, small broad beans or tomatoes.

Gazpacho with Freshwater Crayfish

Gaspacho aux écrevisses

For four people

3kg *(6½ lb)* large freshwater crayfish
400g *(14 oz)* good cucumbers, peeled
150g *(5½ oz)* red pepper
1kg *(2¼ lb)* very ripe tomatoes, peeled, deseeded and diced
olive oil
1–2 tablespoons single cream
3 shallots, chopped
half an onion, chopped
2 cloves of garlic, finely crushed
2–3 sprigs of thyme
1 teaspoon chopped tarragon
a dash of red wine vinegar
200ml *(7 fl. oz)* double cream (optional)
salt, freshly ground pepper

Preparing the gazpacho

Cut the cucumbers in half and scoop out all the seeds. Cut them into chunks, season, and cook gently in a covered saucepan with a little olive oil. Towards the end of the cooking time add a tablespoon or two of cream. When the cucumbers are very soft, purée them in a food processor and set them aside in a bowl.

Grill the red pepper, skin it and remove the seeds. Purée in a food processor and add to the cucumber mixture.

Heat 2–3 tablespoons of olive oil in a saucepan and soften the shallots, onion and garlic. Add the tomato, season with salt and pepper, add the fresh thyme and tarragon, and reduce well.

Cooking the crayfish

Bring a large pan of well-salted water to the boil.

Remove the black intestines of the crayfish by breaking off the central tail fin and drawing it out. The intestine will come with it.

Throw the crayfish into the boiling water and cook them for 2 minutes after the water has come back to the boil. Take the pan off the heat, let it cool for 5 minutes, then lift out the crayfish and refresh them.

Shell the tails and large claws, and reserve them in the refrigerator.

Finishing and serving the gazpacho

Mix the tomato mixture into the cucumber and pepper purée. Taste for seasoning: the soup should have plenty of flavour; add a dash of vinegar and a little olive oil. Stir in some double cream if you want a less Mediterranean flavour.

Ladle into four soup plates, covering the bottoms completely with the purée, which should be rather fluid and velvety, not stiff.

Quickly sauté the crayfish claws and tails in a little olive oil to stiffen them somewhat and to give them a brighter colour, then arrange them on top of the soup.

Crabs Stuffed with Cucumbers

Tourteaux farcis aux concombres

For four people

8 very small or 4 small live crabs

for the court-bouillon
half a bottle of dry white wine
a sprig of thyme
1 bay leaf
1 stick of celery
a small bunch of parsley stalks
1 onion, stuck with a clove

1 cucumber, peeled
coarse salt

for the dressing
½ tablespoon mustard
4 tablespoons double cream or *crème fraîche* (p.23)
1 teaspoon Worcester sauce
a drop of Tabasco
juice of a lemon
3 hard-boiled eggs
1 tablespoon tomato sauce
salt, freshly ground pepper

Cooking the crabs

Put all the ingredients for the *court-bouillon* into a large saucepan and add 3 litres *(5¼ pints)* water. Bring to the boil and cook for 30–45 minutes, then throw in the crabs. Cook for 15 minutes from the moment the liquid comes back to the boil, and let them cool in their liquid.

Open the shells and crack the claws. Extract the crab meat in the usual way, keeping the shells intact. Put the brown meat in a separate bowl to the white, and keep a few larger pieces of white meat for decoration.

Preparing the cucumber

Cut the cucumber in half lengthwise, remove the pips with a teaspoon and cut the flesh into thin, crescent-shaped slices. Sprinkle with coarse salt and leave to salt down for 30 minutes, then drain and pat dry with paper towels.

Dressing the crab

Separate the egg yolks from the whites and set the whites aside. Crush the yolks and mix them with all the remaining ingredients for the dressing.

Incorporate the brown meat from the crabs. Taste for seasoning and mix with the white crab meat and cucumber slices. Fill the cleaned crab shells with this mixture.

Serving the stuffed crabs

Sprinkle the stuffed crabs with the reserved pieces of crab meat and with the egg whites either diced or cut into little strips.

Suggestions

This is a very good but simple dish. The only difficulty lies in extracting the crab meat – avoid getting pieces of shell in the mixture.

Marinated Chicken Alexandre

Marinade de blanc de poularde de Bresse Alexandre

For four people

2 large free-range chickens, weighing 2kg *(4½ lb)* each
4½ litres (1 gallon) clarified stock

for the marinade
250ml *(8 fl. oz)* chicken *demi-glace* or well-reduced clarified stock
2 tablespoons sherry vinegar
2 tablespoons wine vinegar
4 tablespoons olive oil
2 tablespoons oil of arachide
1 generous teaspoon strong mustard
2 cloves
a sprig of thyme
half a bay leaf
½ teaspoon tarragon, chopped
1 shallot, finely chopped
a dash of cognac
juice of half a lemon
salt, freshly ground pepper

100g *(3½ oz)* fine French beans, cooked
1 ripe tomato, peeled, deseeded and cut into quarters
4 slices of truffle
salt, freshly ground pepper

Preparing the chicken

Remove the legs from the chickens and reserve them to use for roasting or for making a fricassee with red wine or a *poulet chasseur*.

Poach the carcasses, with the breasts intact, in clarified stock for 15 minutes. Remove and allow to cool.

Preparing the marinade

Mix all the marinade ingredients together and taste for seasoning. Leave to infuse for 20 minutes and then strain through a fine wire sieve. Chill in the refrigerator.

Marinating and serving the chicken breasts

Remove the chicken breasts from the carcasses and cut each one into three large, thin escalopes. Arrange them in a dish and pour on the marinade. Allow to marinate for several minutes, then remove the breasts and arrange them on four plates, moistening them at the last minute with a little of the marinade and decorating them with the French beans arranged in little bouquets and the quarters of tomato cut into thin crescents. Arrange the slices of truffle on top.

Suggestions

This first course is extremely fresh and appetising; it presents chicken breasts in an original way. They are tender and full of flavour due to the relatively short cooking time.

The decoration can be varied according to the time of year, using a salad of small leaves, fresh asparagus, etc.

Warm Salad of Frogs' Legs with Salmon and Chives

Cuisses de grenouilles en salade tiède et goujonettes de saumon
    sauvage à la ciboulette

For four people

32 frogs' legs
200g *(7 oz)* butter

for the sauce aigrelette

250ml *(8 fl. oz)* mayonnaise, made with three parts oil of arachide
    to one part olive oil
3–4 tablespoons aromatic white wine *court-bouillon* (p.14)
1 teaspoon white wine or sherry vinegar
juice of a lemon
2 tablespoons chives, snipped
½ tablespoon tarragon, chopped

600g *(1 lb 5 oz)* salmon fillet, boned
a few sprigs of chervil and dill
salt, freshly ground pepper

Cooking the frogs' legs

Cook the frogs' legs gently in butter for about 8 minutes, seasoning them
generously with salt and pepper. When they are tender allow them to cool
and then bone them carefully, keeping them as nearly as possible in their
original shape. Set aside in a stainless-steel pan, moistened with a little of
their cooking liquid.

Preparing the *sauce aigrelette*

The consistency of this sauce should be much more liquid and lighter than
mayonnaise. Add all the ingredients, adjusting them until you are satisfied
with the flavour and have a sauce which will coat lightly without sticking. Add
the herbs.

Preparing the salmon

Heat the oven to its highest setting. Cut the salmon into 8–12 pieces about the
size of a finger. Put them on a buttered oven dish and keep them ready.

Pour some of the sauce over the frogs' legs and heat them gently, stirring
continuously.

Meanwhile, sprinkle the pieces of salmon lightly with water and put them into
the oven. They will take about 2–3 minutes to cook.

95

Serving the frogs' legs and salmon salad

Put a little pyramid of warm frogs' legs in their sauce in the centre of four heated soup plates. Pour the remaining sauce round the sides and arrange a few pieces of salmon on top, two or three to each plate. Decorate with sprigs of chervil and dill and serve straight away.

Sautéed Frogs' Legs with Parsley and Garlic

Cuisses de grenouilles sautées aux fines herbes

For four people

800g *(1¾ lb)* frogs' legs
400g *(14 oz)* butter
2 tablespoons parsley and garlic, finely chopped
a little flour
salt, freshly ground pepper

If you can find fresh frogs' legs, knot them together. Dip them into flour just before cooking, as you would for a sole *meunière*.

Melt about 80g *(3 oz)* butter in each of two large frying pans. Put in the frogs' legs and season generously. When they start to brown lightly, turn them over one at a time with a carving fork. Lower the heat and continue to cook the frogs' legs until they are golden brown but not dried up; do not let the butter brown too much.

In a nice oval *gratin* dish, melt the remaining butter until it foams. Put in the drained frogs' legs and sprinkle with the parsley and garlic. Serve at once.

Suggestions

Cooking frogs' legs in butter is quite a delicate business. It is important not to let them dry out, so watch them carefully. Add a little fresh butter if the frying butter is getting too dark.

Truffled Sausage in Beaujolais Cooked on the Hearth

Cervelas truffé au beaujolais sous la cendre

For six people

1 truffled cervelas sausage
1 bottle Beaujolais
aluminium foil

Buy a large truffled cervelas sausage (or one with pistachio nuts) from a good butcher, delicatessen or charcuterie.

Make a large cone out of aluminium foil and put in the sausage. Pour in the Beaujolais and seal the parcel hermetically so that the wine won't run out.

Carefully place the parcel in a hole hollowed out in the embers of a good low fire, and cover the top over with more embers.

Leave for an hour, then retrieve the parcel and open it over a deep dish. The smell is a treat in itself.

Serve it cut into slices with some good coarse country bread and butter, and – obviously – a bottle of cool Beaujolais.

Suggestion
You could use a large fresh truffled sausage instead of the cervelas.

Georges Blanc's Sea-bass with Marinière Sauce

Bar de ligne à la marinière Georges Blanc

For four people

1 sea-bass, weighing 1kg *(2¼ lb)*
1 litre *(1¾ pints) sauce marinière* (p.16), freshly made
50g *(2 oz)* butter
sprigs of chervil
salt, freshly ground pepper

97

Preparing the bass

Pre-heat the oven to its highest setting.

Remove the fillets from each side of the fish, so that you have two large fillets. Remove the bones and slice each one into little slices about ½cm *(¼ in)* thick. Butter an oven dish or baking sheet and arrange the escalopes of bass on it side by side.

Heat the *sauce marinière* and taste it for seasoning.

Cooking and serving the bass

Just before serving, season the slices of bass lightly and moisten them slightly by sprinkling them with water. Slide them into the hot oven and watch carefully – the water will be turned into steam and the fish will cook extremely rapidly (in fact almost immediately). Remove quickly, making sure the fish is done by sliding a spatula underneath it and looking to see if the underside is cooked.

Arrange the pieces of fish on four large heated plates. Cover generously with the sauce and sprinkle with sprigs of chervil. Serve at once.

Suggestions

Make sure the fish is very fresh. This recipe can be used for other fish or shellfish, according to what is in the market or whatever you feel like buying that day – you could perhaps do a mixture of fish and lobster or Dublin Bay prawns or scallops.

Ragoût of Snails with Wild Mushrooms

Ragoût d'escargots de Bourgogne forestière

For four people

4 dozen large snails, cooked in *court-bouillon*
2 shallots, chopped
250g *(8½ oz)* wild mushrooms (chanterelles or St George's mushrooms), cleaned and chopped
60g *(2 oz)* butter
1 large tomato, skinned, deseeded and diced
100ml *(4 fl. oz)* double cream or *crème fraîche* (p.23)
20g *(¾ oz)* garlic butter (p.48)
salt, freshly ground pepper

Heat the snails in a saucepan in some of their cooking liquid, or in salted water if this is not available.

Soften the chopped shallots in plenty of butter for a few minutes, then add the chopped mushrooms and sweat them for 5 minutes. Add the chopped tomato and the drained snails. Stir them into the mushroom mixture, then add the cream. Reduce until lightly thickened. Finish by adding the garlic butter.

Taste for seasoning and serve in small individual dishes, either enamelled iron or porcelain.

Suggestions

You could use large Burgundy snails or the more ordinary, smaller *petit gris*. If using fresh snails rather than preserved ones, make certain they are thoroughly cooked.

Snails in Red Wine Sauce with Mushrooms

Escargots de Bourgogne en meurette

For four people

4 dozen snails, freshly cooked or tinned *'au naturel'*
1 bottle strong red wine

for the sauce
3 shallots, chopped
2 cloves of garlic, crushed
a sprig of thyme
1 bay leaf
1 teaspoon *beurre manié* (a little flour worked into a nut of butter)
1–2 tablespoons meat glaze

300g *(10½ oz)* small button mushrooms (or chanterelles)
1 tablespoon butter
120g *(4½ oz)* small onions, skinned
100g *(3½ oz)* smoked streaky bacon
2 slices white bread, crusts removed, and diced
1 tablespoon parsley, chopped
salt, freshly ground pepper

Preparing the sauce

Pour the red wine into a saucepan and add the vegetables and herbs for the sauce. Simmer until the wine has reduced by two-thirds, remove the flavourings with a slotted spoon and stir in a little *beurre manié* – enough to give the sauce a velvety consistency. Cook for a further 5 minutes, then add the meat glaze to enrich the flavour, and taste for seasoning.

Preparing the garnish

Slice the mushrooms fairly thickly and sauté them briefly in a little butter. Remove, drain and set aside. Cook the cubes of bread to a golden brown in butter. Drain. Cook the onions in boiling salted water until tender. Drain well. Cut the bacon into little strips and blanch them for a minute or two in boiling unsalted water. Drain.

Finishing and serving the snails

Add the snails to the red wine sauce together with the mushrooms, small onions and bacon, and heat through. Blend in about 30g *(1½ oz)* butter cut into small pieces to perfect the flavour and texture of the sauce, and spoon into little individual dishes. Sprinkle with the small croûtons and the chopped parsley, and serve at once.

Suggestions

This dish can be served either as a first course or, by slightly changing its character, as a main course. In the latter case, increase the quantity of mushrooms, serve it in soup plates as if it were a ragoût, placing a poached egg in the middle of each plate at the last moment.

The flavour of the sauce in this good peasant dish depends on the quality of the wine used for the sauce.

Little Soup-Herb Tarts

Petite tarte aux herbes potagères

For four people

for the pastry
125g *(4½ oz)* plain flour
70g *(2½ oz)* butter
1 egg yolk
100ml *(4 fl. oz)* milk (approximately)
½ teaspoon salt
5 slender leeks
2 large new onions
50g *(2 oz)* butter
4 spinach leaves, cut into ribbons
2 sorrel leaves, cut into ribbons
a small bunch of chives, snipped
4 tablespoons thick double cream
salt, freshly ground pepper

Preparing the pastry

Prepare the pastry in the usual way, using the ingredients listed above and adding only as much liquid as is necessary to make a good dough. Let it rest in the refrigerator for at least an hour or so.

Preparing the soup herbs

Remove the outside leaves from the leeks. Split the leeks and wash them well, then slice them very finely.

Skin the onions, cut them in half and slice them finely.

Melt the butter in a sauté pan and soften the onions and leeks very gently, without browning. Season with salt and pepper, and cook for 15 minutes.

Add the spinach and sorrel leaves and the snipped chives, and cook, still over a low heat, for a further 5 minutes. This mixture should be soft and tender.

Add half the cream, let it reduce a little, and taste for seasoning.

Pre-heat the oven to Reg. 8/450°F/230°C.

Cooking, filling and serving the tarts

Pre-heat the grill.

Butter a jam-tart tin. Roll out the pastry and cut out 8–12 rounds. Line the tart moulds and prick the bottoms. Fill each one with aluminium foil, or whatever you usually use to stop pastry rising. Cook for 12–15 minutes in the hot oven and, when they are done, remove and fill with the hot herb mixture.

Whisk the remaining cream in a bowl and cover the tops of the tarts with it. Glaze quickly under the hot grill and serve at once.

Suggestions

A nice, easily made and inexpensive first course. You can use other herbs, such as chervil or tarragon, in the making of this dish, or add very small lardons of blanched bacon to the herb mixture.

Casserole of Dublin Bay Prawns with Herbs and Mushroom Flans

Etuvée de grosses langoustines aux herbes et gâteau de
   champignons

For four people

20–28 large, very fresh Dublin Bay prawns
200g *(7 oz)* mushrooms (a mixture of cultivated, chanterelles, St
   George's mushrooms, etc.)
1 whole egg
1 egg white
1 shallot, finely chopped
6 tablespoons double cream or *crème fraîche* (p.23)
150g *(5½ oz)* butter
juice of 1 or 2 lemons
½ tablespoon tarragon, chopped
6 tablespoons whipping cream (optional)
a few chive tips for decoration
salt, freshly ground pepper

Preparing the Dublin Bay prawns

Rinse the shellfish in fresh running water, and then cut the heads from the tails. Discard the heads, and shell the tails by twisting the shells so that the flesh is separated and can be drawn out whole. You could do this by cutting the shells with scissors instead. Make a shallow incision along the tops of the tails and remove the black intestine. The tails are now ready to be cooked. Keep them in a cold place.

Preparing the mushroom flans

Pre-heat the oven to Reg. 2/300°F/150°C.

Clean the mushrooms and cook them for a few minutes in boiling salted water. Drain them well and reduce them to a fine purée in a liquidiser or food processor.

Transfer the mushrooms to a bowl and work in the egg and egg white, the finely chopped shallot and the cream. Season the mixture and divide it between four little buttered moulds.

Cook for 10–15 minutes in the low oven. Test for doneness by inserting a skewer or the point of a small knife into the middle. Keep them hot until you are ready to turn the flans out of the moulds.

Making the whisked butter sauce

Bring 2 tablespoons of water to the boil in a shallow saucepan and gradually whisk in 100g *(3½ oz)* of the butter, cut into dice, whisking vigorously to obtain a velvety sauce. Season, add the juice of 1 lemon (more if necessary) and the chopped tarragon, and whisk in more butter or a few tablespoons of cream to perfect the texture of the sauce.

Finishing and serving the casserole

Melt the remaining 25g *(1 oz)* butter in a large sauté pan over a brisk heat. Throw in the shellfish and cook them for 1–2 minutes until they become firm.

Turn out the mushroom flans on to four very hot plates, arrange the shellfish tails all round and coat lightly with the tarragon sauce. Decorate with chives and serve at once.

Suggestions

If the Dublin Bay prawns are very large they can be cut in half lengthwise, after they are cooked, and arranged on the plates cut-side down to improve the look of the dish.

Serve with a white wine from a good vineyard – a Pouilly-Fuissé, a Meursault or a Chassagne-Montrachet.

Richard Cressac's Sole with Black Olives and Anchovy Sauce

Timbale de sole Richard Cressac à l'anchois et aux olives noires

For four people

250g *(8½ oz)* small mussels
50g *(2 oz)* black olives, stoned
2 tomatoes, skinned, deseeded and diced
4 fillets of sole, skinned
2 shallots, chopped
150g *(5½ oz)* butter
100ml *(4 fl. oz)* dry white wine
juice of half a lemon
250ml *(8 fl. oz)* double cream or *crème fraîche* (p.23)
a little anchovy essence
a pinch of curry powder (optional)
sprigs of chervil and chive tips
salt, freshly ground pepper

Preliminary preparations

Wash and scrape the mussels thoroughly. Cut the stoned olives into rounds.

Wash the fillets of sole and cut them across into strips 2cm *(¾ inch)* wide. Place them side by side on a buttered oven dish. Reserve in a cool place.

Pre-heat the oven to its hottest setting.

Making the sauce

Soften the shallots in a nut of butter, and when they are tender add the white wine and throw in the mussels. Cover and cook for 5 minutes or until the mussels are all open.

Shell the mussels and strain their cooking liquid through a fine sieve.

Melt the remaining butter and add a squeeze of lemon juice.

Put the mussels' cooking liquid in a small saucepan and reduce by half. Add the cream, and reduce again until velvety and slightly thickened. Stir in the anchovy essence – as much or as little as you like. Put the sauce in a liquidiser to give it a very smooth, light, creamy texture.

Cooking and serving the sole

Sprinkle the strips of sole lightly with water and slide them into the oven for 3–4 minutes.

Meanwhile, finish the sauce by adding the melted butter and, if you like, a pinch of curry powder. Taste for seasoning and add the diced tomato, the mussels and the olives. Heat through.

When the sole is cooked, divide the pieces between four heated plates. Remove the pieces of tomato, the mussels and the olives from the sauce with a slotted spoon and garnish the sole with them. Coat lightly with the sauce and decorate with sprigs of chervil and chive tips.

Fillets of Salmon Trout with Vegetable Brunoise and Port

Filets de truite saumonée à la brunoise de légumes et au porto

For four people

4 salmon trout, weighing 300g *(10½ oz)* each, or 2 larger salmon
  trout, weighing 700g *(1½ lb)* each
1 carrot ⎫
1 small turnip ⎪
50g *(2 oz)* celeriac ⎬ all cut into very small dice *(brunoise)*
1 small courgette ⎭
6 small onions, finely chopped
6 shallots, finely chopped
1 *bouquet garni* of parsley stalks, thyme and half a bay leaf
80g *(3 oz)* butter
6 **tablespoons** sweet white wine (Sauternes, Barsac or
  Monbazillac)
2 **tablespoons** port
6 **tablespoons** aromatic white wine *court-bouillon* (p.14) or
  fish fumet (optional)
juice of half a lemon
1 large tomato, skinned, deseeded and diced
1 **tablespoon** continental parsley, coarsely chopped
salt, freshly ground pepper

Preparing the *brunoise*

Melt 50g *(2 oz)* of the butter in a *gratin* dish and put in the diced vegetables. Add the *bouquet garni* and cook gently for about 5 minutes, stirring the vegetables round with a wooden spoon. Season them with salt and pepper as they are cooking. Deglaze the pan with the sweet white wine and the port, and the aromatic white wine *court-bouillon* or fish fumet if you have it.

105

Preparing the salmon trout

Cut each fish into two large fillets and season each fillet on both sides. Pre-heat the oven to Reg. 4/350°F/180°C.

Place the fillets on top of the *brunoise* of vegetables, cover with aluminium foil, and cook until just done – 6–10 minutes. Watch the trout carefully, as their flesh is very delicate and must not be over-cooked. By the time they are ready, the vegetables should be tender. Lift out the trout fillets and put them on a serving dish.

Finishing and serving the salmon trout

Drain the vegetables in a sieve placed over a small saucepan and reduce the cooking liquid over a brisk heat until you have a shiny, velvety sauce. Add the remaining butter, cut into pieces, and a squeeze of lemon juice. Taste for seasoning.

Add the *brunoise* to this sauce, together with the diced tomato, and coat the fillets of salmon trout lavishly with this sauce. Sprinkle with the chopped parsley and serve at once.

Chicken Breasts 'Club des Cent'

Chaud et froid de poularde de Bresse 'Club des Cent'

For four people

2 free-range chickens, weighing about 2kg *(4½ lb)* each

for the chicken stock
4 carrots
4 shallots
2 cloves of garlic
4 onions
1 leek
2 sticks of celery
1 clove
a sprig of thyme
1 bay leaf
1 chicken stock cube (optional)

a pinch of curry powder
100ml *(4 fl. oz)* dry white wine
250ml *(8 fl. oz)* double cream or *crème fraîche* (p.23)
a generous dash of port
½ teaspoon Dijon mustard

for the garnish
2 tomatoes, skinned, deseeded and diced
100g *(3¹/₂ oz)* fresh green peas, shelled before weighing
100g *(3¹/₂ oz)* small broad beans, podded before weighing
100g *(3¹/₂ oz)* small silver onions, peeled
20g *(³/₄ oz)* truffle and its juice
salt, freshly ground pepper

Cooking the chicken breasts

Remove the legs from the chickens and set them aside to use on another occasion (in a fricassee, for example, or for roasting).

Put all the ingredients for the chicken stock into a large pan, add enough water to cover the two chicken carcasses when they go in later, bring it to the boil and simmer for half an hour.

Put in the chicken carcasses with their breasts intact and simmer for 20 minutes. Lift them out, remove the fillets with a sharp knife and keep them hot, wrapped in aluminium foil.

Making the sauce

Chop up the carcasses with a heavy knife or cleaver and brown them in butter in a sauté pan. Remove the vegetables and herbs from the chicken stock with a slotted spoon and add them to the carcasses.

Add a pinch of curry powder and the white wine, reduce by half and then add the cream and a dash of port. Season with pepper and salt and stir in the mustard and truffle juice.

Cook gently until the sauce is smooth and velvety and then strain into a small pan and keep hot.

Preparing the garnish

Cook the peas and the broad beans separately in boiling salted water and skin the broad beans. Cook the onions in boiling salted water and then glaze them in butter with a little icing sugar. Cut the truffle into julienne strips.

Serving the chicken

Just before serving, slice the chicken breasts with a flexible knife and arrange them in fans on four heated plates. Coat lightly with the sauce, well seasoned, and scatter the small vegetables and the truffle julienne decoratively over the top. Serve at once.

Suggestions

Take care with the cooking of the chicken breasts – they should be very juicy and tender. The sauce should have plenty of flavour to enhance the chicken.

The garnish of small vegetables gives the dish a delicate touch.

Freshwater Crayfish with Fresh Herbs and Beurre Blanc

Petite marmite de queues d'écrevisses aux aromates

For four people

2–2½kg *(4½–5½ lb)* live freshwater crayfish
50g *(2 oz)* butter

to garnish the crayfish

1–2 carrots, cut into julienne strips
1 leek, white part only, cut into julienne strips
1 stick of celery, cut into julienne strips
1 teaspoon each of basil, tarragon and parsley, chopped
1 teaspoon chives, snipped
1 teaspoon chervil sprigs
50g *(2 oz)* butter

for the court-bouillon

2 litres *(3½ pints)* dry white wine
1 litre *(1¾ pints)* water
300g *(10½ oz)* carrots, cut into pieces
2–3 onions, cut into quarters
1 stick of celery, cut into pieces
1 lemon, peeled *à vif* and sliced
1 *bouquet garni*
70g *(2½ oz)* salt
15g *(½ oz)* whole peppercorns

for the beurre blanc

2 shallots
1 tablespoon white wine vinegar
4 tablespoons dry white wine
3 tablespoons thick double cream
150g *(5½ oz)* butter, cut into dice
juice of half a lemon
salt, freshly ground pepper

Preliminary preparations

Sweat the julienned vegetables lightly in butter, in a covered pan, until just tender. Set them aside.

Cook all the ingredients for the *court-bouillon* together in a large pan for 20 minutes. Strain and return to the pan.

Making the *beurre blanc*

Put the shallots in a medium saucepan with the vinegar and white wine. Boil rapidly until the liquid has almost completely evaporated, then add the cream and cook gently until it has reduced by half. Whisk the butter into this mixture, a piece at a time, whisking continuously to emulsify the sauce. Taste for seasoning and keep warm.

Cooking the crayfish

Bring the *court-bouillon* to the boil and remove the intestines from the crayfish (p.91). Drop them into the *court-bouillon* and cook them for 2 minutes from the time the *court-bouillon* returns to the boil. Drain and shell them.

Sauté the crayfish tails rapidly in butter to make them firmer, then moisten them with a little of their *court-bouillon,* and add the julienne of vegetables and all the chopped herbs. Heat almost to simmering point, then at the last moment add the *beurre blanc* and a few drops of lemon juice.

Taste the sauce for seasoning and divide the crayfish, vegetables and sauce between four small heated dishes.

Suggestions

The cream in this sauce makes it possible to heat the *beurre blanc* to a higher temperature.

You can garnish this dish in other ways – with small new vegetables or mushrooms such as chanterelles or St George's mushrooms. You could serve it in soup plates instead of little individual dishes.

Gratin of Love-apples

Gratin de pommes d'amour

For four people

1½kg *(3½ lb)* rather ripe, handsome tomatoes
2 cloves of garlic
thick double cream
2 tablespoons chervil and parsley, finely chopped
salt, freshly ground pepper

Pre-heat the oven to Reg. 6/400°F/200°C.

Choose ripe tomatoes, not too large, and skin them by plunging them for a few seconds into boiling water and then into cold water. The skins can then be easily removed.

Cut the tomatoes in half, removing the pips and the hard part by the stalk. Cook them gently in a covered pan with a few tablespoons of water for about 4–5 minutes. Drain well.

Rub the inside of a large *gratin* dish with the two cloves of garlic and arrange the tomatoes in it. Season them well. Spoon the cream over the top.

Bake in the oven until the top is a nice golden colour. Sprinkle with the chopped herbs and serve very hot.

Grilled Slip Soles
with Courgettes in Cream

Céteaux grillés aux courgettes à la crème

For four people

12 slip soles, skinned but left whole
a little flour
200g *(7 oz)* butter
6 tablespoons oil of arachide
2 onions, finely chopped
1kg *(2¼ lb)* courgettes, finely sliced
4 tablespoons double cream
4 tablespoons grated Gruyère (optional)
salt, freshly ground pepper; a pinch of nutmeg

Preparing the courgettes

Soften the onions in 3 tablespoons of oil of arachide. When they are almost tender, add the courgettes and season with salt and pepper. Cover the pan and simmer for 15 minutes, then remove the lid and cook until the liquid has evaporated.

Preparing and serving the soles

Dip the soles lightly in flour, tap them to get rid of any excess, and then fry them in butter with 3 tablespoons of oil of arachide until they are golden and just cooked through – about 3 minutes on each side.

Just before serving, add the cream and grated Gruyère to the courgettes and adjust the seasoning, adding a generous pinch of nutmeg. Serve as a garnish to the fried slip soles.

Suggestion

Use small new courgettes, or you could use tiny cherry tomatoes.

Steamed Monkfish with Red Pepper Vinaigrette

Lotte à la vapeur et à la vinaigrette de poivrons doux

For four people

800g–1kg *(1³/₄–2¹/₄ lb)* monkfish fillets

for the vinaigrette
6–8 tablespoons olive oil
1–2 tablespoons sherry vinegar
1½–2 teaspoons herb mustard

2 cloves of garlic, finely chopped
half a red pepper, cut into small dice
1 tablespoon chives, finely snipped
2 handfuls of seaweed for steaming
salt, freshly ground pepper

Make the vinaigrette in the normal way (see p.37).

Cut the monkfish into fine slices, allowing three or four slices per person. Steam them over boiling water, laying them on a bed of seaweed in the top of the steamer. They will need 3–4 minutes' cooking time according to how thick they are.

111

Meanwhile warm the vinaigrette gently with the garlic and diced red pepper. Divide the pieces of monkfish between four heated plates and sprinkle generously with the vinaigrette. Scatter the chives over the top at the last moment and serve warm.

Suggestions

You could serve this simple dish with a few little new potatoes, cooked in boiling salted water and sliced as for a potato salad. Serve them arranged round the monkfish and bathed in the same vinaigrette.

Sweetbreads with Sorrel

Ris de veau à l'oseille

For four people

1kg *(2¼ lb)* firm rounded sweetbreads, trimmed
1 large handful of sorrel, cut into fine shreds
150g *(5½ oz)* butter
flour for the sweetbreads
100ml *(4 fl. oz)* dry white vermouth
1 tablespoon meat glaze (optional)
250ml *(8 fl. oz)* double cream
salt, freshly ground pepper

Preparing the sweetbreads

Prick the sweetbreads with a trussing needle and leave them in a bowl under a trickle of cold running water for an hour or two. Transfer them to a saucepan of cold salted water, bring to the boil and blanch for 10 minutes, stirring them round once or twice.

When they have whitened, remove from the heat and blanch them under cold water. Trim away any fatty parts and fibres. Cut into slices 1cm *(½ in)* thick and reserve.

Cooking the sweetbreads

Shortly before you are ready to serve them, dip the slices of sweetbread lightly into the flour, tapping them to remove any excess.

Meanwhile, heat half the butter in a large frying pan and brown both sides of the sweetbreads rapidly. Then turn down the heat to finish cooking, without drying them out. Season them with salt and pepper and transfer them to a large heated serving dish. Keep hot.

Making the sauce and serving the sweetbreads

Pour the butter out of the frying pan and deglaze the pan with the vermouth, stirring and scraping the bottom of the pan to dissolve the caramelised juices. Add the meat glaze and then the cream, bring the sauce to the boil and reduce it a little. Taste for seasoning and add the remaining butter, cut into pieces. Add more cream, or even a little *beurre manié*, if the sauce seems too liquid.

Strain the sauce through a fine sieve into a small pan and add the raw sorrel, cut into ribbons. Heat the sauce through and pour it over the sweetbreads on their serving dish. (Do not boil the sauce after adding the sorrel.)

Suggestion

You could use the same recipe to cook lambs' sweetbreads.

Beef Paupiettes Stuffed with Red Peppers and Tomatoes

Oiseaux sans tête farcis aux poivrons et à la tomate

For four people

600g *(1 lb 5 oz)* beef skirt or sirloin, cut into four large, thin slices
2 red peppers
3 tablespoons olive oil
4–5 tomatoes, skinned, deseeded and diced
a clove of garlic, crushed
100g *(3½ oz)* smoked streaky bacon, cut into fine lardons
a sprig of fresh thyme
1 shallot, chopped
100ml *(4 fl. oz)* strong red wine
1 teaspoon tomato purée
salt, freshly ground pepper, a pinch of cayenne

Preparing the stuffing

Pre-heat the oven to Reg. 2/300°F/150°C. Put the peppers on a lightly oiled baking sheet and cook them for 20 minutes, then skin them and remove the seeds. Cut them into strips and sauté them in a tablespoon of oil. Add the tomatoes, the crushed clove of garlic, the lardons of bacon, previously fried in a little oil, and the thyme leaves stripped from the stalk. Reduce until all the water has evaporated and you have a sort of purée.

113

Stuffing the *paupiettes*

Spread out the slices of beef on a board and season them with salt, pepper and a little cayenne.

Spoon a quarter of the stuffing on to each slice in such a way that you can then roll up the beef, folding the slices in to form a small parcel enclosing the stuffing. Tie with string.

Heat the remaining olive oil in a small casserole and brown the four *paupiettes*. Add the shallot, and when the *paupiettes* are brown all over add the red wine and tomato purée, and let the liquid reduce by half. Then add the same quantity of water, cover the pan and simmer for 20 minutes. Remove the string and serve very hot.

Suggestions

The sauce should be well flavoured and not too liquid. Sieve it, if necessary, and add a little butter to give it a gloss if you like.

Serve the *paupiettes* with saffron rice or plain boiled rice, perhaps scattered with strips of stoned black olives.

You could make the same dish with veal escalopes or chicken breasts.

Sautéed Lamb with Almonds and Aubergines

Sauté d'agneau aux amandes et aubergines

For six people

1½kg *(3½ lb)* shoulder of lamb, boned and cut into large, even
  pieces
150ml *(¼ pint)* olive oil
1 *bouquet garni*
1 clove of garlic
a few coriander seeds
a pinch of saffron
3 aubergines, cut into large rectangular pieces (skins left on)
100g (3½ oz) blanched almonds, coarsely chopped
2 large spring onions, sliced
1 tablespoon butter
salt, freshly ground pepper

Heat half the oil in a large frying pan and brown the pieces of lamb all over. Transfer them to a casserole with a slotted spoon, draining off all the oil and patting them dry with paper towels. Season them with salt and pepper and add the herbs, garlic and spices. Add just enough water to cover the meat, and simmer for 30–40 minutes.

Fry the aubergines in the remaining olive oil, barely letting them brown, then drain on paper towels.

Sweat the almonds and onions in a tablespoon of butter and add them and the aubergines to the lamb 10 minutes before the end of the cooking time.

Serving the lamb

If the sauce is too liquid, remove the pieces of lamb and vegetables to a hot dish with a slotted spoon. Reduce the sauce, return the lamb and its accompanying vegetables, taste for seasoning and serve very hot.

Suggestions

You could also include tomato in the sauce. If the sauce with its melting vegetables does not seem fluid enough, you can add a little fresh olive oil, some consommé or even a little water.

Ham with a Rich Sauce of Cream and Mushrooms

Jambonneau à la crème aux mousserons

For four people

2 cooked knuckles of ham or 1 small, boned, rolled foreleg of gammon, previously soaked and cooked
150g *(5½ oz)* St George's mushrooms
1 tomato, cut into quarters
200g *(7 oz)* diced carrot, onion, shallot (mirepoix)
1 small bouquet garni
100g *(3½ oz)* salt belly of pork or streaky bacon, diced
100g *(3½ oz)* butter
500ml *(16 fl. oz)* clarified stock or 275ml *(9 fl. oz)* white wine
500ml *(16 fl. oz)* double cream or *crème fraîche* (p.23)
1 tablespoon port
a dash of brandy
2 tablespoons whipped cream
salt, freshly ground pepper

115

Preliminary preparations

Trim and wash the mushrooms. Dry them well and set them on one side.

Heat the cooked hams, whole, in a covered pan containing a little salted water (unsalted if the ham is salty).

Preparing the sauce

While the ham is heating, melt half the butter in a sauté pan and put in the tomato, mirepoix of vegetables, herbs and diced belly of pork or streaky bacon. When everything is turning a beautiful pale golden colour, add the stock or white wine. Simmer to reduce by half, add the cream and then reduce by half again.

Strain the sauce through a fine sieve. Adjust the consistency and flavour by adding a little port and a dash of brandy. Season to taste with salt and pepper.

Finishing and serving the ham

Pre-heat the grill.

Just before serving, sauté the mushrooms in the remaining butter. Drain the hot ham and pat it dry. Remove the skin and slice the ham into fairly thick slices. Arrange them on a large heated serving dish.

Drain the mushrooms and add them to the sauce. Add a little whipped cream, taste for seasoning and coat the slices of ham lightly with the sauce, arranging the mushrooms over the top.

Slide the dish under the hot grill and glaze it lightly to a pale golden colour. Serve at once.

Suggestion

Serve this ham with leaf spinach cooked in butter, seasoned with salt, pepper and a little nutmeg, and flavoured with a single clove of garlic.

Veal Piccata with Lemon and Courgette Flans

Piccata de veau au citron et flan de courgettes

For four people

8 little medallions of veal, prepared by the butcher (taken from the fillet)
2 tablespoons flour, sifted
50g *(2 oz)* butter
2 tablespoons olive oil
3–4 tablespoons dry white wine
zest and juice of 2 lemons
1 ripe tomato, skinned, deseeded and cut into large dice
200ml *(7 fl. oz)* double cream or *crème fraîche* (p.23)
salt, freshly ground pepper

for the courgette flans

4 medium courgettes, diced
3 eggs
500ml *(16 fl. oz)* double cream or *crème fraîche* (p.23)
salt, freshly ground pepper, grated nutmeg

Preliminary preparations

Pre-heat the oven to Reg. 2/300°F/150°C.

Flatten the medallions of veal with a cutlet beater or large, heavy knife blade.

Cut the lemon zest into julienne strips and blanch them in boiling water for 1 minute.

Making the courgette flans

Butter four little dariole moulds. Cook the diced courgette for 5 minutes in boiling salted water and then drain them very well, pressing them to extract excess juices. Purée them in a liquidiser.

Mix the courgette purée in a bowl with the eggs and cream, and season the mixture with salt, pepper and nutmeg. Transfer the mixture to the buttered moulds and cook for 20 minutes.

Cooking the veal

Season the medallions with salt and pepper and dip them lightly in flour, tapping off any excess. Heat the butter and oil in a large sauté pan and brown them evenly on both sides. When they are a rich golden brown, but not yet cooked, take them out of the pan and keep them warm. Pour away most of the fat.

117

Add the white wine to the pan, scraping up all the caramelised juices, and then add the lemon juice and diced tomato. Return the medallions and add 3–4 tablespoons of water. Simmer for 5–6 minutes, then remove the pieces of veal, arrange them on four heated plates and keep them hot.

Finishing the sauce and serving the veal

Reduce the sauce a little, add the cream and reduce again until velvety. Taste for seasoning and pour the sauce over the veal. Sprinkle with the blanched lemon zest, and serve with the little courgette flans turned out on one side of the plate.

Suggestions

Be careful not to make the sauce too lemony. You could give it added flavour by adding a little pinch of curry powder.

You could replace the courgette flans with a flan made with the green parts of Swiss chard leaves, chopped, and the stalks cooked *au gratin*.

Daube of Beef in Jelly

Daube en gelée

For eight people

2kg *(4½ lb)* top rump of beef, cut into 3–4cm *(1½–2 in)* cubes
2 calves' feet, blanched and cut into four pieces
250g *(8½ oz)* smoked streaky bacon, cut into lardons

for the marinade
3 shallots, coarsely sliced
a clove of garlic, unpeeled
500ml *(16 fl. oz)* dry white wine
1 *bouquet garni*
2 tablespoons olive oil

2 tablespoons olive oil
250g *(8½ oz)* fresh white onions, sliced
500g *(1 lb 2 oz)* carrots
250g *(8½ oz)* shelled green peas
250g *(8½ oz)* fine French beans
a few sprigs of flat parsley
2 tomatoes, skinned, deseeded and quartered
salt, freshly ground pepper, grated nutmeg

Two days before: marinating the beef

Put the beef, calves' feet and the streaky bacon into a large bowl with all the ingredients for the marinade, and marinate in a cool place for 24 hours.

The day before: cooking the beef

The next day, pat the meat dry and brown it in 2 tablespoons of fresh olive oil. When it is a golden brown all over, add the calves' feet, the lardons of bacon, the marinade, the sliced onions and half the carrots, sliced into rounds. Add enough water just to cover the meat, and bring to the boil. Simmer, covered, for 2–3 hours. The meat is done when it is easily pierced with a fork.

Cooking the vegetables

While the meat is cooking, cook the peas, the beans (cut into little dice) and the rest of the carrots (also cut into dice) separately in boiling salted water.

Assembling the *daube*

When it has cooled, put a layer of one-quarter of the beef in an oiled terrine, followed by a layer of all the peas, then another layer of beef, then the carrots, then beef, followed by a layer of all the beans and lastly a layer of beef.

Reduce the cooking liquid somewhat, taste it for seasoning and then strain it over the meat and vegetables in the terrine. Cover with greaseproof paper and a weighted board that just fits into the terrine. Refrigerate for 12 hours. Put any leftover liquid in a dish to set.

On the day: serving the beef

Turn the *daube* out on to a serving dish and surround it with the jellied cooking liquid, cut into cubes, the quarters of tomato and little bunches of parsley.

Suggestions

Serve this *daube* in the summer with a *sauce tartare* or fresh tomato sauce (p.12) — in which case omit the tomatoes from the decoration.

Chicken
with Tarragon Vinegar and Cream Sauce

Poulet de Bresse au vinaigre

For four people

1 large free-range chicken, weighing 1.6–1.8kg *(3½–4 lb)*
100g *(3½ oz)* butter
3 carrots, cut into large pieces
5 small onions or 1 large onion, cut into four
3 cloves of garlic, unpeeled
100ml *(4 fl. oz)* tarragon vinegar
200ml *(7 fl. oz)* clarified chicken stock
2 sprigs of fresh tarragon
1 teaspoon mustard
2 teaspoons flour
1 teaspoon tomato purée
500ml *(16 fl. oz)* double cream
6 tablespoons fresh tomato sauce (p.12)
salt, freshly ground pepper

Preparing and cooking the chicken

Pre-heat the oven to Reg. 8/450°F/230°C.

Cut the chicken into eight pieces (two drumsticks, two thighs, two breasts and two wings). Fry them in butter in an enamelled iron casserole. Add the carcass, chopped into three pieces, and brown the pieces of chicken evenly all over, seasoning them with salt and pepper. Add the carrots, onions and garlic and cover the casserole. Cook in the hot oven for 30 minutes, adding a tablespoon of vinegar after 15 minutes, so that the fumes can be absorbed by the chicken.

Making the sauce

Take out the pieces of chicken and keep them hot. Skim the fat off the cooking juices and add the rest of the vinegar, a little at a time. Add the chicken stock, tarragon, the flour mixed with a little liquid, the mustard and tomato purée, and reduce, stirring. Then add the cream and reduce again until the sauce is velvety.

Serving the chicken

Strain the sauce through a fine sieve and add the fresh tomato sauce. Arrange the pieces of chicken on a serving dish and coat them with the sauce.

Suggestions

Serve with rice.

The quality of the chicken is as important in this dish as the flavour of the cooking juices, which give the sauce its succulence. The pieces of chicken must therefore be fried carefully with plenty of butter. Large chickens over 2kg *(4¹/₂ lb)* are excellent for this recipe, but then you will need more liquid and flavourings.

You can prepare this dish ahead, keeping the pieces of chicken covered with a more liquid sauce. If it becomes too dry, add more water or cream.

Chicken with Seven Vegetables in Pistou Sauce

Fondue de poularde au pistou

For four people

1 good free-range chicken
2 litres *(3¹/₂ pints)* strong clarified chicken stock

for the macedoine

2 leeks
2 carrots
1 onion
1 stick of celery
2 cloves of garlic
1 fresh fennel twig

60g *(2 oz)* butter
3 tablespoons olive oil
2 sprigs of fresh thyme
1 bay leaf
3 tomatoes, skinned, deseeded and diced
2–3 tablespoons *pastis*
2 tablespoons flour
1 tablespoon each basil and tarragon, chopped
a pinch of saffron
2 tablespoons thick double cream
3 potatoes, turned into little barrel shapes (the size of garlic cloves)
salt, freshly ground pepper

Cooking the chicken

Poach the cleaned chicken in the stock for half an hour, then turn off the heat and let it sit in its cooking liquid.

Preparing the vegetables

Cook the potatoes in some of the chicken's cooking liquid. Cut all the vegetables for the *macedoine* into small dice. Heat the butter and half the oil and sweat the vegetables gently, adding the bay leaf, thyme and diced tomatoes. Flame them with the *pastis* and stir in the flour. Moisten gradually with some of the cooking liquid from the chicken to obtain a little light sauce which bathes the vegetables. Cook gently for 15–20 minutes, adding more liquid if necessary. Add a little more *pastis* and a tablespoon of olive oil if necessary. Stir in the basil, tarragon and saffron and taste for seasoning. Keep hot.

Finishing and serving the chicken

Drain the chicken, skin it and remove the bones. Cut it into even pieces the size of a sugar-lump – they must be very regular. Fold them carefully into the vegetables and add the cream and a little more butter.

Incorporate the potatoes, divide the mixture between four hot soup plates and serve very hot.

Suggestions

Suitable as a main course, this dish should be very well flavoured and is full of tastes that underline the quality of the chicken. Take care to keep the sauce light and to cut the vegetables and chicken neatly. At different seasons of the year you can add different vegetables – such as peas, broad beans, etc. – for a more complicated dish.

Little Mousses of Red Mullet with Bouillabaisse Sauce

Mousseline de rouget sauce bouillabaisse

For four people

600g *(1 lb 5 oz)* fillets of red mullet
a pinch of *quatre épices* (p.58)
a pinch of cayenne
½ teaspoon freshly ground black pepper
4 egg whites
500ml *(16 fl. oz)* double cream or *crème fraîche* (p.23)
1 litre *(1¾ pints)* bouillabaisse sauce (p.20)
salt

Making the mousse

Purée the filleted, boned and skinned red mullet in a food processor and then rub it through a fine sieve to obtain a perfectly smooth mixture. Add the spices and salt and then the egg whites, one at a time. Whisk the cream lightly and fold it into the mixture carefully with a wooden spatula. Taste for seasoning. Heat the bouillabaisse sauce.

Cooking the mousses

Pre-heat the oven to Reg. 2½/310°F/160°C.

Butter four individual soufflé dishes or moulds and fill them three-quarters full with the mousse mixture. Cook them in a bain-marie in the oven for about 30 minutes. Watch them carefully and test by inserting a trussing needle into the centre of the mousse – when it comes out clean they are done. Let them rest a few minutes before turning them out on to small soup plates. Serve them hot, lightly coated with hot bouillabaisse sauce.

Suggestions

If you like you can give this dish a more elaborate presentation by surrounding the mousses with little bouquets of shellfish tails (either freshwater crayfish cooked in *court-bouillon* or Dublin Bay prawns gently stewed in butter).

You could also serve it more simply with a light *beurre blanc* flavoured with fresh herbs (p.11), or a Sauternes sauce with curry powder (p.21).

Best End of Lamb with Mushroom Sauce and Courgette Flans

Filet d'agneau à la crème de champignons, gâteau de courgettes et tomates

For four people

1.2–1.5kg *(about 3 lb)* loin or best end of lamb in a piece containing 8 ribs
5 cloves of garlic, peeled

for the courgette flans

1 leek, trimmed
4 courgettes, cut into large pieces
3 cloves of garlic
1 egg
2 egg whites
4 tablespoons double cream or *crème fraîche* (p.23)

2 shallots
1 carrot
a sprig of thyme
4 ripe tomatoes, skinned and cut into 8 sections
3 tablespoons olive oil
150g *(5½ oz)* butter
a bunch of watercress
salt, freshly ground pepper
250ml *(8 fl. oz) sauce forestière* (p.19)

Preparing the lamb

Bone the lamb so that you have a well-shaped fillet. Season it, roll it up and tie it with string into a neat shape. Cut two cloves of garlic into slivers and push these into little incisions made with a sharp knife in the lamb. Keep the bones to roast with the lamb.

Pre-heat the oven to Reg. 2½/310°F/160°C.

Making the courgette flans

Bring a pan of salted water to the boil and cook the leek, three cloves of garlic and the courgettes for about 20 minutes. Drain well, pressing the vegetables to extract all the excess water and then purée them in a food processor, incorporating the egg, egg whites and cream. Season the mixture and divide it between four well-buttered individual soufflé dishes or ramekins. Cook in a bain-marie for 20–25 minutes. When they are ready, keep them hot and turn up the oven to its highest setting.

Cooking the lamb fillet

Brown the lamb fillet gently on all sides in a little butter. Transfer it to a roasting tin with a large nut of butter, a clove of garlic, the shallots, carrot and a sprig of thyme. Put in the lamb bones and roast rapidly for 10–12 minutes. Test the lamb by pressing it with your finger; keep it slightly blue in the middle. Put it to relax in a warm place for 10 minutes, well covered, turning it over frequently.

Preparing the cooking juices

Skim the fat off the cooking juices and deglaze the pan with a little water. Whisk in the remaining butter, cut into pieces, to make a velvety sauce. Keep it warm.

Serving the lamb

Pour some of the *sauce forestière* over the bottom of four very hot plates. Unmould one of the courgette flans in the centre of each.

Slice the lamb, allowing two or three slices for each person, and arrange them round the green flans on top of the sauce. In between arrange the sections of tomato, like the petals of a flower. Coat lightly with the cooking juices and decorate each plate with a small bunch of watercress.

Suggestions

Although this dish has several different elements, the flavours all harmonize perfectly. Great care should be taken with presentation, which is particularly pleasing to the eye.

You can, if you like, add a small panful of different wild mushrooms sautéed lightly in butter; arrange them round the courgette flans.

Resting the meat gives it an even, rosy tone all the way through.

The fillet of lamb can be marinated in the refrigerator with herbs and flavourings and some olive oil for 2–3 days. It will then be even more tender and well flavoured.

Fillet of Turbot
with Sorrel and Beurre Rouge

Filet de turbot au beurre rouge et à l'oseille

For four people

1 chicken turbot, weighing 2kg *(4½ lb)*
8 Dublin Bay prawns (shelled raw)
500ml *(16 fl. oz)* strong, well-rounded red wine

for the fumet
3 shallots
2 carrots
2 onions
1 stick of celery
2 cloves of garlic
1 tomato
1 clove
a sprig of thyme
1 bay leaf
parsley stalks

a walnut-sized piece of *beurre manié*
1 tablespoon meat glaze
half a lemon
150g *(5½ oz)* butter
4 leaves of sorrel, finely shredded
salt, freshly ground pepper

Preparing the fish and the fumet

Have the turbot filleted and keep the bones. Reserve the fillets in a cool place. Bring the wine to the boil in a saucepan and flame it. Add 250ml *(8 fl. oz)* of water. Wash and chop up the fish bones.

Melt a little butter in a separate pan and add the ingredients for the fumet. Sweat them for a minute or two, then add the turbot bones and head. After a further 2 minutes of gentle cooking add the wine, bring it to the boil and let it simmer for 30 minutes.

Heat the oven to its hottest setting.

Making the sauce

Strain the fumet and reduce it by a third. Stir in the *beurre manié*, then add the meat glaze and a dash of lemon juice.

Cooking the turbot

Melt 30g *(1 oz)* of butter in a large frying pan and put in the turbot fillets, cut into eight nice pieces. Start them off on top of the stove and give them a quick glazing on each side. Then transfer the pan to the oven and cook for a further 3–4 minutes. Remove them, drain them carefully and arrange them on four heated plates. Keep hot.

Finishing and serving the turbot

Add the remaining butter in little pieces to the red wine sauce, whisking it in well to obtain a velvety finish to the sauce. Taste for seasoning. Sauté the Dublin Bay prawn tails rapidly in a little extra butter in a non-stick frying pan. Arrange two for each person on top of the turbot, after coating the turbot lightly with the red wine sauce. Sprinkle the very finely shredded sorrel over the sauce and serve at once.

Suggestions

All sorts of firm white fish can be cooked as a main course in this way. Take great care over the red wine sauce – it should be well flavoured and velvety.

Raspberry Sorbet

Sorbet framboise

For four people

500g *(1 lb 2 oz)* raspberries
1 lemon
150g *(5½ oz)* sugar
150ml *(¼ pint)* water

Choose very ripe, perfect raspberries with a rich flavour. Remove the seeds by pressing them through the fine blade of a *mouli-légumes*.

Melt the sugar in the water, bring it up to boiling point, and then let it cool.

Mix the raspberry juice with the cold syrup and the juice of a lemon, strain it through a fine sieve and freeze in a sorbetière.

Suggestions

Although this excellent sorbet can be kept for a few weeks in a freezer, it is best freshly made and served in a glass decorated with a few fresh raspberries.

Iced White Peach Soup with Redcurrant Juice and Mint

Soupe glacée de pêches blanches au jus de groseille à la menthe

For four people

6 large ripe white peaches, heavily scented
200g *(7 oz)* sugar
250ml *(8 fl. oz)* water
300g *(10½ oz)* redcurrants, removed from their stalks
1 lemon

Make a syrup by dissolving the sugar in the water over a medium heat. Allow it to cool.

Extract the pips from the redcurrants using the fine blade of a *mouli-légumes*.

128

Stir the redcurrant juice into the syrup and add the juice of a lemon. Strain this syrup through a fine sieve.

Skin the peaches and cut them into six or eight slices. Arrange in a dish and cover them with the redcurrant syrup.

Chill in the refrigerator. Serve very cold in soup plates or bowls.

Suggestions

You could add a generous scoop of vanilla or mint ice-cream to each plate, placing it in the centre of the peaches, or you could simply decorate the soup with fresh mint leaves.

Little Honeyed Madeleines

Petites madeleines au miel

For eight people

100g *(3½ oz)* ground almonds
250g *(8½ oz)* icing sugar
100g *(3½ oz)* flour
8 egg whites
250g *(8½ oz)* butter
1 generous tablespoon honey

Mix the ground almonds, icing sugar and flour together in a bowl, and add the egg whites one at a time, mixing in each one thoroughly before adding another.

Melt the butter in a frying pan until it turns a clear hazelnut colour, then pour it into the mixture and mix it in lightly but thoroughly. Add a generous tablespoon of honey.

Let the mixture rest in the refrigerator for one hour.

Pre-heat the oven to Reg. 6–7/400–425°F/210–220°C. Put the mixture into well-buttered madeleine tins and bake until a good pale golden colour.

Suggestions

If possible, serve these madeleines while they are still warm – they will be all the more irresistible.

Use miniature madeleine tins if you can, so that each is no more than one mouthful, crisp on the outside.

Redcurrant and Almond Tart

Tarte aux groseilles et à l'amande

For four people

for the sweet flan pastry
200g *(7 oz)* flour
100g *(3½ oz)* sugar
100g *(3½ oz)* butter
1 whole egg

120g *(4½ oz)* redcurrants, stalks removed
1 tablespoon ground almonds
2 tablespoons fine brown sugar
5 tablespoons double cream or *crème fraîche* (p.23)

Make the sweet flan pastry and let it rest for 20 minutes in the refrigerator.

Pre-heat the oven to Reg. 4/350°F/180°C.

Roll out the pastry and use it to line a buttered tart ring placed on a baking sheet.

Prick the bottom of the tart all over with a fork and put in an even layer of redcurrants.

Mix the almonds, sugar and cream in a bowl and cover the redcurrants with this mixture. Put the tart in the pre-heated oven and bake for about 15–20 minutes. Take it out when the bottom of the tart is cooked, and serve, preferably cold.

Suggestions
You can add a few shelled walnuts, left over from the previous autumn. The redcurrants will burst as they cook and colour the tart a beautiful pink with their juice.

Iced Mousse with Oranges, Raspberries and Strawberries

Mousse glacée aux fruits rouges et à l'orange

For eight people

10 egg yolks
250ml *(8 fl. oz)* whipping cream, whipped until firm
1kg *(2¼ lb)* oranges
500g *(1 lb 2 oz)* raspberries and strawberries
200ml *(7 fl. oz)* water
300g *(10½ oz)* sugar

Making the mousse (the night before)

Dissolve the sugar in the water in a saucepan and boil for 3 minutes. Whisk the egg yolks in a bowl with a whisk or electric beater. Pour the syrup slowly into this mixture, whisking all the time. Continue to whisk until the mixture becomes light and creamy; it will take about 10–15 minutes. Fold the mixture into the whipped cream and freeze.

Finishing and serving the mousse

Peel the oranges *à vif*, removing every shred of pith. Divide into segments, cutting inside the white skin that divides one piece from another so that each segment is completely skinless.

Hull the strawberries and cut them in half.

Just before serving, chill eight bowls or soup plates, then put two nicely shaped scoops of mousse in the centre of each. Arrange the orange segments, strawberries and raspberries alternately all round the edge.

Suggestions

To give the mousse more character, add a dash of liqueur or *eau-de-vie*, rum, Grand Marnier or *eau-de-vie de framboise* – according to how you feel. You can also serve it with fresh raspberry or strawberry sauce poured over the fruit.

Zabaglione of White Peaches with Sauternes and Wild Strawberries

Sabayon de pêches blanches au sauternes et aux fraises des bois

For four people

4 perfectly ripe white peaches
4 egg yolks
40g *(1¹/₂ oz)* sugar
150ml *(¹/₄ pint)* sweet white wine (Sauternes or Barsac)
juice of half a lemon
icing sugar
a few mint leaves
125g *(4¹/₂ oz)* wild strawberries

Making the zabaglione
Mix the egg yolks, sugar and wine in a shallow saucepan. Whisk over a very low heat until you have a light and foamy zabaglione of a pale yellow colour. It will take about 5 minutes.

Preparing the peaches
Pre-heat the grill.

Wash and dry the peaches and cut each one into eight slices. Arrange them in circles, radiating out like the spokes of a wheel, on four large heated soup plates.

Finishing and serving the peaches
Whisk the zabaglione mixture with the lemon juice and spread it over the peaches. Sprinkle with icing sugar and glaze under the hot grill. Scatter the wild strawberries over the top and decorate with a fresh mint leaf. Serve at once.

Suggestions
If the peaches are very ripe it is better not to peel them.

Wild strawberries can be replaced with raspberries, and you could serve the zabaglione with a spoonful of fresh raspberry sauce underneath the peaches.

Floating Island with Pralines

Ile flottante aux prâlines

For eight people

14 egg whites
a pinch of salt
350g *(12 oz)* sugar
100g *(3½ oz)* crushed pralines (p.80)

for the custard

1 litre *(1¾ pints)* milk
1 vanilla pod
250g *(8½ oz)* caster sugar
10 egg yolks

Making the island

Whisk the egg whites with a pinch of salt and 150g *(5½ oz)* of the sugar until you have a firm snow, then gradually incorporate the rest of the sugar. Fold in the crushed pralines at the last moment. Pre-heat the oven to Reg. 2/300°F/150°C.

Butter a large soufflé dish at least 8–10cm *(3–4 in)* deep and sprinkle the inside with caster sugar. Fill it with the meringue mixture, place it in a bain-marie and cook in the oven for about 20 minutes. The island is cooked when the meringue will no longer stick to your finger when lightly touched.

Take it out of the oven, allow it to cool and turn it out into the middle of a deep serving dish.

Making the custard

Bring the milk to the boil in a saucepan with the split vanilla pod and 100g *(3½ oz)* of the caster sugar; let it infuse for at least 5 minutes.

Put the egg yolks in a large mixing bowl, add the remaining sugar and whisk for several minutes until the mixture becomes very pale and creamy. Pour on the milk in a thin stream, whisking energetically all the time.

Return this mixture to the pan and heat gently, stirring continuously with a wooden spatula or whisk. When you see the very first signs of simmering, the custard is ready. It should lightly coat the back of the spatula. Strain it and let it cool.

Serving the floating island

Serve with the custard poured round the island and offer sponge biscuits or small brioches, or perhaps a slice of chocolate cake, to accompany it.

Rice with Apricots

Gâteau de riz aux abricots

For eight people

1kg *(2¼ lb)* fresh apricots cooked in syrup or 750g *(1 lb 10 oz)*
   tinned apricot halves in their syrup
50g *(2 oz)* lump sugar
200g *(7 oz)* pudding rice (round grain)
1½ litres *(2½ pints)* milk
2 vanilla pods, split
60g *(2 oz)* butter, cut into small pieces
4 egg yolks, lightly beaten

Making the caramel

Dissolve the lump sugar in the apricot syrup in a heavy-bottomed saucepan. Boil until the syrup caramelises, then pour it into a charlotte mould, swirling it round so that it lines the bottom and sides completely.

Cooking the rice

Wash the rice, rinsing it under the cold tap, then drain it well and cook it in the milk, together with the vanilla pods, until tender. It must be perfectly done, tender but not mushy: it takes about 10 minutes. Test it frequently.

Making the mould

Stir the butter into the rice a little at a time, then add all the egg yolks, beaten with a fork. Transfer the rice to the caramelised mould, cool and leave to set for at least 3 hours in the refrigerator.

Serving the mould

Turn out the mould carefully on to a serving dish and surround it with the apricot halves.

Suggestions

Serve on its own or with custard, a caramel sauce or an apricot sauce.

Do not try to use anything but round-grain rice for this recipe.

Autumn

Salad of Dublin Bay Prawns with Saffron and Wild Mushrooms

Salade de langoustines au safran et aux champignons

For four people

20 large, very fresh, raw Dublin Bay prawns
4 handfuls of salad leaves in season (red raddichio, lamb's lettuce,
   frizzy endive, rocket, etc.)
150g *(5¹/₂ oz)* wild mushrooms (ceps, chanterelles, St George's
   mushrooms, etc.)
100g *(3¹/₂ oz)* butter
1 tablespoon olive oil
a pinch of saffron strands
3 tablespoons vinaigrette (p.45)
40g *(1¹/₂ oz)* truffles, cut into julienne strips (optional)
sprigs of chervil
salt, freshly ground pepper

Preliminary preparations

Wash the Dublin Bay prawns and remove the heads. Shell the tails, cutting through or breaking the rings of the tail shell to extract the meat; this is one of the rare shellfish that is easy to shell. Reserve in a cool place.

Wash the salads; take care to have some that are tender and some that are crisp. Dry them carefully, using a cloth if necessary. Reserve in a salad bowl.

Trim and wash the mushrooms, cutting larger ones into pieces, and cook for 10 minutes in boiling salted water; test to see if they are done by pinching them. Drain and set aside.

Cooking the Dublin Bay prawns and mushrooms

Heat 50g *(2 oz)* of the butter in a frying pan with the oil. Throw in the Dublin Bay prawn tails and season them with salt and pepper. Cook them for 1–2 minutes, turning them over frequently, until they lose their translucent look. They mustn't brown or overcook. Add a few saffron strands – not too much – and remove the pan from the heat.

Add a further 50g *(2 oz)* butter in little pieces to bring the juices to a velvety consistency. Keep warm.

At the same time, cook the mushrooms in butter in a separate frying pan. Drain and keep hot.

137

Dressing and serving the salad

Toss the salad briefly with the vinaigrette and arrange it in little domed mounds on four plates. Arrange Dublin Bay prawns and mushrooms alternately round the sides of the salad and coat them lightly with the saffron butter. Decorate with the truffle julienne and scatter sprigs of chervil over the salads. Serve at once.

Suggestions

If the Dublin Bay prawns are really large, cut them in half lengthwise after cooking. The cut surface will have a very appetising pearly sheen. You could add a few little dice of ripe tomato for the colour.

Artichoke Hearts with Chicken Livers in Foie Gras Sauce

Fonds d'artichauts aux foies blonds sauce foie gras

For four people

8 small purple artichokes
juice of half a lemon
1 tablespoon flour
100g *(3½ oz) foie gras* or purée of *foie gras*
6 tablespoons double cream
1 teaspoon port
8 large pale chicken livers
200g *(7 oz)* lamb's lettuce or rocket
100ml *(4 fl. oz)* vinaigrette (p.45)
15g *(½ oz)* butter
1 truffle, cut into julienne strips (optional)
salt, freshly ground pepper

Preliminary preparations

Pare the artichokes with a small sharp knife, removing all the leaves and keeping only the hearts. Cook them in boiling salted water to which you have added the lemon juice and flour. When they are tender, remove the prickly chokes with a teaspoon.

Flatten the chicken livers somewhat by tapping them with a large, heavy knife blade so that they cook evenly and do not contract as they cook.

138

Making the *foie gras* sauce

Press the *foie gras* through a sieve and whisk it with the cream in a small saucepan over a very low heat. Season with salt and pepper and finish the sauce by adding a dash of port. Keep warm.

Preparing the salad

Wash the salad and pick it over carefully. Dry it in a cloth and at the last moment, just before serving, dress it with some of the vinaigrette and arrange a flat rosette of leaves on each of four plates.

Slice the artichoke hearts thinly, sprinkle them with the rest of the vinaigrette, put them back into their original shape, but slightly tipped to one side, and place them in the middle of the salad.

Cooking and serving the chicken livers

Season the livers with salt and pepper, then fry them in a little butter to a good golden-brown colour without overcooking them. They should still be slightly pink inside. Arrange them on the salads, around the artichoke hearts, and coat lightly with the slightly warm *foie gras* sauce. Decorate with the julienne of truffles.

Paupiettes of Smoked Salmon with Dublin Bay Prawns

Pannequet de saumon farci aux langoustines

For four people

400g *(14 oz)* finely sliced smoked salmon
12 large raw Dublin Bay prawns
500ml *(16 fl. oz)* mayonnaise
1 teaspoon green herb mustard
juice of half a lemon
a few tablespoons of aromatic white wine *court-bouillon* (p.14)
15g *(½ oz)* butter
1 tomato, skinned, deseeded and diced
a few chives
sprigs of dill or chervil
salt, freshly ground pepper

Preliminary preparations

Shell the Dublin Bay prawns, discarding the heads. Remove the black intestines by making a shallow slit along the back of each one. Wash and dry them and set them aside in a cool place.

Prepare the mayonnaise and season it well. Stir in the green mustard and a few drops of lemon juice, and lighten it with a few tablespoons of *court-bouillon*. It should just coat the back of a spoon without feeling sticky to the touch.

Preparing the Dublin Bay prawns

Cook the Dublin Bay prawn tails in a little butter until they are just firm and without letting them brown. Season them, deglaze the pan with a little of the *court-bouillon* and cook very briefly – the shellfish should be firm and have lost their translucent appearance, but should not be cooked for long. Cut each one in half lengthwise, and coat the pieces lightly with some of the green mayonnaise.

Making the salmon *paupiettes*

Spread out the slices of smoked salmon on a board and put some of the Dublin Bay prawns down the centre of each slice so that it can be rolled up like a stuffed pancake. Cut each roll into lengths of about 8cm *(3 in)*, allowing three rolls to each person.

Finishing and serving the *paupiettes*

Cover the bottoms of four plates lightly with the green mayonnaise. Arrange the *paupiettes*, pointing outwards like sunrays, on top. Decorate them with pieces of tomato, chive tips and sprigs of dill or chervil.

Suggestion

The Dublin Bay prawns could be replaced by little strips of scallop cooked in *court-bouillon* (p.14).

Terrine of Foie Gras Marinated in Port

Terrine de foie gras d'oie mariné au porto

For four people

1 or 2 *foie gras*, preferably goose, weighing 700–800g *(1²/₃–1³/₄ lb)*
  each
15g *(¹/₂ oz)* salt
8g *(¹/₄ oz)* freshly ground pepper } per 1kg *(2 lb)* of *foie gras*
a pinch of *sel rose*
a pinch of *quatre épices* (p.58)
a pinch of grated nutmeg
1 bottle of port
100ml *(4 fl. oz)* Armagnac

Make the terrine several days ahead.

Preparing the *foie gras* (the day before cooking)
Choose very fine-quality livers and if they seem very stiff soak them for a short
time in warm water to soften them. Then pat them dry and carefully remove
the central veins, separating the two lobes.

Remove all the little strings and nerves, cutting them away carefully with a
small knife. Take care not to handle the livers too roughly – they should keep
their original shape. Leave as much of the very fine skin that covers them as
possible.

Weigh the livers and put them into a deep dish. Add the salt and spices and
cover the livers with the port and Armagnac. Gently move them around in the
liquid so that the seasonings are evenly distributed. Cover with greaseproof
paper and leave to marinate in the refrigerator for at least one day.

Cooking the *foie gras*
Remove the livers some time before you want to cook them, so that they can
warm up to room temperature.

Pre-heat the oven to Reg.¹/₄/175°F/80°C.

Choose an enamelled cast-iron or white porcelain terrine, with a lid, which is
the right size for the quantity of livers you are going to cook. Put in the lobes
resting on their outer surfaces; press them down gently. They can slightly
overfill the terrine so that it will be filled to the brim when they have cooked.
Put the lid on and cook in a bain-marie for 1½ hours. Test by piercing with a
trussing needle, plunging it into the centre of the livers; when placed on the
tongue, the heat should be just perceptible.

Finishing the *foie gras*

Remove from the oven and allow to cool, pressing lightly with a board that just fits into the terrine. Keep, covered, in the refrigerator for several days before serving.

To keep the terrine longer, make it air-tight by pouring some goose fat (or, failing that, lard) over the top to seal it.

Serve with toast, preferably made with coarse country bread.

Suggestions

You can also use this recipe to cook duck *foie gras*, but make sure they are the best quality; the seasoning and timing are crucial to their success, as they are more delicate.

It is also possible to put a line of truffles down the middle of the terrine before cooking it. Make a delicious, well-seasoned, port-flavoured jelly to accompany the *foie gras* if you like.

Smoked Haddock with Spinach

Filet de haddock aux épinards

For four people

2 smoked haddock fillets, trimmed
500ml *(16 fl. oz)* milk
750g *(1 lb 10 oz)* spinach
200ml *(7 fl. oz)* classic *beurre blanc* (p.11)
100g *(3½ oz)* butter
a pinch of grated nutmeg
a clove of garlic, peeled
salt, freshly ground pepper

Poach the haddock in the milk for 6–10 minutes, according to how thick the fillets are.

Wash the spinach and blanch it in boiling salted water for 5 minutes. Drain, refresh and drain again very carefully, on a cloth if possible.

Prepare the *beurre blanc.*

Cook the spinach gently in the butter with the nutmeg and clove of garlic. Divide it between four heated plates and place the smoked haddock, cut into four pieces, on top. Strain the *beurre blanc* over the top, sprinkle with freshly ground pepper and serve hot.

Suggestions

You could serve the smoked haddock on a bed of raw spinach. In this case, replace the *beurre blanc* by a well-flavoured vinaigrette with fresh herbs in it and a poached egg on top.

Frogs' Legs with Cream and Shallots

Cuisses de grenouilles à la crème échalotée

For four people

1kg *(2¼ lb)* frogs' legs
2 tablespoons flour
200g *(7 oz)* butter
3 shallots (preferably 'grey-skinned'), finely chopped
500ml *(16 fl. oz)* thick double cream
2 tablespoons chives, finely snipped
juice of half a lemon
salt, freshly ground pepper

Preparing the frogs' legs

Wash the frogs' legs, knot them and pat them dry with a cloth or paper towels. Just before cooking, dip them lightly in flour, tapping to remove any excess.

Cooking the frogs' legs

Melt a large nut of butter over a brisk heat in a black iron frying pan (use two pans if you prefer). When the butter is hot but not brown, put in the frogs' legs, seasoning them with salt and pepper. Cook the frogs' legs, turning them over and adding a little fresh butter to stop the cooking butter from browning. Then turn down the heat so that the frogs' legs do not dry out.

Finishing and serving the frogs' legs

After 3–4 minutes, throw in the chopped shallots. Let them simmer for a moment, then add half the cream. Stir gently and simmer gently for several minutes, adding the rest of the cream to give the sauce a smooth, velvety texture.

Add the chives and a squeeze of lemon juice at the last moment. Taste for seasoning and serve in a large heated serving dish.

Suggestions

This simple rustic dish is easily made. It is best to serve it in two helpings so that it can be eaten very hot.

Dublin Bay Prawns with Leeks

Etuvée de langoustines à la fondue de poireaux

For four people

24 large, very fresh, raw Dublin Bay prawns
3 large leeks, white parts only
100g *(3½ oz)* butter
150ml *(¼ pint)* aromatic white wine *court-bouillon* (p.14) or
    light fish stock
300ml *(½ pint)* double cream or *crème fraîche* (p.23)
2–3 tablespoons *beurre blanc* (p.11)
juice of half a lemon
fresh tarragon, chervil and chives for decoration
salt, freshly ground pepper

Preparing the Dublin Bay prawns

Shell the Dublin Bay prawns raw, removing the heads, and take out the black intestines by making a shallow incision along the backs of the tails with a small, sharp knife. Reserve in a cool place.

Cooking the leeks and the shellfish

Cut the leeks into fine julienne strips and stew them gently in butter for 15 minutes. Season them with salt and pepper and keep covered with a round of greaseproof paper.

At the last moment, sauté the shellfish tails in a very little butter in a non-stick frying pan, letting them stiffen for about 1 minute. Moisten with the *court-bouillon* and cook, covered, for a further minute.

Finishing the sauce and serving the 'stew'

Remove the leeks and spread them over the bottom of four heated soup plates. Using a slotted spoon, divide the Dublin Bay prawns between the four plates and keep them hot.

Reduce the cooking liquid by half, add the cream and reduce again until you have a sauce that coats the back of the spoon lightly. Add 2 tablespoons of *beurre blanc* and a squeeze of lemon juice. Taste for seasoning, make certain the sauce is smooth and velvety, and spoon it over the shellfish. Decorate with the fresh herbs.

Suggestions

Take care not to overcook the shellfish – it would spoil the dish.

The leeks could be replaced by some other vegetable – a variety of green purées, leaf spinach, wild mushrooms, a julienne of different vegetables, etc.

145

Warm Salad of Scallops with Tarragon

Salade tiède de coquilles Saint-Jacques à l'estragon

For four people

16 scallops in their shells
250ml *(8 fl. oz)* aromatic white wine *court-bouillon* (p.14)
mayonnaise, made with 60ml *(2 fl. oz)* olive oil and 180ml
  (6 fl. oz) oil of arachide
juice of half a lemon
1–2 teaspoons tarragon, chopped
a few salad leaves, cut into ribbons *(chiffonade)*
1 stick of celery, finely sliced
salt, freshly ground pepper

Preparing the scallops

Open the scallops and wash them carefully, removing the beards and all the sand. Keep only the white parts, detaching them from their shells with a spoon. Cut them horizontally into two or three rounds, depending on how thick they are.

Cooking the scallops

Prepare the aromatic white wine *court-bouillon* and let it simmer for 20 minutes. Throw in the scallops and allow them to simmer gently for 3 minutes from the time the liquid comes back to simmering point. Drain them and strain the *court-bouillon*.

Cut the scallops across into generous batons, and put them into a salad bowl.

Dressing and serving the salad

Add some of the strained *court-bouillon* and the juice of half a lemon to the mayonnaise, making it more liquid. Pour it over the scallops and stir in the chopped tarragon. Taste for seasoning and arrange in little mounds on four plates or individual dishes, on top of the *chiffonade* of salad leaves and a scattering of sliced celery.

Suggestions

The mayonnaise should not be too liquid, just relaxed enough to coat the back of a spoon lightly. If you think tarragon may be too overpowering, replace it with chervil.

You can give the salad an extra touch with little dice of tomatoes, a julienne of truffles, or perhaps chive tips or samphire spears.

Scallops with Ceps and Soy Sauce

Saint-Jacques aux cèpes sauce soja

For four people

16 scallops
250g *(8¹/₂ oz)* fresh ceps
1 tablespoon olive oil
100ml *(4 fl. oz)* dry white wine
200ml *(7 fl. oz) beurre blanc* (p.11)
1 teaspoon soy sauce
juice of half a lemon
sprigs of chervil for decoration
salt, freshly ground pepper

Preparing the scallops

Choose large fresh scallops, open them, discarding the beards, and wash them well in cold water. Detach them from their shells and cut them in half horizontally if they are very large. Arrange them on a lightly buttered *gratin* dish. Heat the oven to its hottest setting.

Preparing the ceps

Trim, wash and dry the ceps, and slice them neatly. Shortly before serving, sauté them in a little oil in a frying pan until they are golden but still firm. Season them, drain off the oil and keep them hot.

Cooking the scallops

Sprinkle the scallops lightly with water and put them straight into the oven, without seasoning them. Allow them to cook for 3–4 minutes; you can test them by pressing with your finger.

Making the sauce and serving the scallops

Add a little white wine to the *beurre blanc* and stir in the soy sauce and lemon juice. Balance the sauce by adding more or less of the different ingredients until it is to your taste. It should be very light and fluid. Add a tablespoon of water if necessary, seasoning again to restore the flavour.

Arrange the scallops on four small heated dishes or a large heated serving dish, arrange the ceps round them and coat lightly with the soy-flavoured sauce. Decorate with sprigs of chervil and serve at once.

Suggestions

You could use the white wine, reduced, in making the *beurre blanc*, and add a dash of vinegar to the sauce at the end, if you liked. You could also cook the scallops with a nut of butter in a non-stick frying pan, taking care not to let them get too brown.

This sauce would be a harmonious accompaniment to a steamed lobster or crawfish sliced into neat rounds.

Ragoût of Scallops with Pistachio Nuts

Ragoût de coquilles Saint-Jacques aux pistaches

For four people

12 large scallops in their shells
1 tablespoon butter
2 shallots, chopped
100ml *(4 fl. oz)* Sauternes or other sweet wine
250ml *(8 fl. oz)* whipping cream
100ml *(4 fl. oz)* whisked butter (p.11)
a pinch of curry powder
juice of half a lemon
50g *(2 oz)* pistachio nuts, skinned
salt, freshly ground pepper

Preparing the scallops

Choose large fresh scallops; open them either with a knife or by placing them rounded side down in a heated oven for a moment, when they will open of their own accord. Remove the beards, washing the scallops well in cold water. Detach them from their shells, cutting them in half horizontally if they are very thick.

Place them on a lightly buttered baking sheet. Reserve in a cool place.

Pre-heat the oven to its highest setting.

148

Making the sauce

Melt a tablespoon of butter in a small saucepan. Add the shallots, let them sweat for a moment, then add the sweet wine. Let it reduce by half, then add the cream. Reduce again and add the whisked butter.

Season the sauce and whisk it well. Add a pinch of curry powder (not too much, as it mustn't be overpowering) and the juice of half a lemon. Taste for seasoning and strain through a fine wire sieve. Keep it hot while you cook the scallops.

Cooking and serving the scallops

Sprinkle the scallops lightly with water and cook them in the hot oven for about 3 minutes. If they are very fresh their juices will caramelise beneath them. Meanwhile, heat the pistachio nuts in hot water.

When the scallops are done, place them caramelised side up on four heated soup plates and coat lightly with the sauce. Scatter the pistachio nuts over the top.

Suggestions

To enhance this dish, decorate the plates with sprigs of chervil, the tips of thin chives, small dice of fresh tomato or little lozenges of carrot cooked in water. By providing a contrast in colour, the garnish adds to the charm and delicacy of the dish.

Oyster Soup with Wild Mushrooms

Soupe d'huîtres aux cèpes et mousserons

For four people

2 dozen oysters (natives or Colchesters, size 1 or 0)
250g *(8½ oz)* ceps, St George's mushrooms, chanterelles, pieds
    de moutons or other wild mushrooms
50g *(2 oz)* butter
1 shallot, finely chopped
6 tablespoons aromatic white wine *court-bouillon* (p.14) or
    very light fish stock
250ml *(8½ fl. oz)* double cream or *crème fraîche* (p.23)
a squeeze of lemon juice
1 tablespoon chives, snipped
a few sprigs of chervil
salt, freshly ground pepper

149

Preparing the oysters

Open the oysters and put them with their juice in a sauté pan, taking care to remove any particles of broken shell and sand. Strain the juice if necessary.

Making the soup

Slice the mushrooms and sauté them in butter with the chopped shallot. Let them brown very lightly, add the *court-bouillon* or fish stock, then add the cream. Cook for a few minutes to reduce the soup slightly. Keep hot.

Cooking the oysters

Just before you are ready to serve the soup, put the oysters in their pan over a low heat and remove them as soon as the liquid shows signs of simmering. Stir a tablespoon of the oyster juices into the mushroom soup and add a squeeze of lemon juice. Add a little butter, cut into pieces, and the snipped chives. Taste for seasoning.

Divide the oysters between four heated soup plates and spoon the very hot soup over them. Scatter the sprigs of chervil over the top as a garnish.

Suggestions

Allow for the flavour of the oysters' cooking liquid when seasoning the soup: it adds a strong, salty, iodine flavour.

Marennes Oysters in Green Waistcoats

Huîtres de Marennes en verdure

For four people

24 large Marennes or other oysters (preferably size 0)
500ml *(16 fl. oz) beurre blanc* with cream (p.11)
2 generous handfuls of large spinach leaves (24 leaves)
2 tablespoons fresh tomato dice
a small pinch of curry powder
a squeeze of lemon juice
salt, freshly ground pepper

Preliminary preparations

Open the oysters and put them with their juice in a sauté pan, taking care to remove any particles of shell and grit.

Wash the spinach and remove any coarse stalks. Blanch in boiling water, removing the leaves as the water returns to the boil, and refresh them in cold water. Spread them out on several plates; you will need twenty-four leaves, one for each oyster.

Cooking the oysters

Bring the oysters and their juice slowly up to simmering point. Remove at once and drain them. Snip off the beards, place each oyster in the middle of a spinach leaf and roll it up into a little cigar-shaped parcel.

Arrange six oysters on each of four heated soup plates, radiating out from the centre like the spokes of a wheel. Place a little bunch of concasséed tomato in the centre of each.

Finishing the sauce and serving the oysters

Reduce the oyster juices and strain them through a very fine sieve. Add the *beurre blanc* and a pinch of curry powder. Taste for seasoning, add a squeeze of lemon juice and coat the oysters lightly with the sauce.

Suggestion

Keep the sauce rather light, to underline the delicacy of this dish.

Alain Detain's Freshwater Crayfish with Snails

Cassolette d'écrevisses aux escargots Alain Detain

For four people

2kg *(4½ lb)* large freshwater crayfish (about 40)
2 litres *(3½ pints)* aromatic white wine *court-bouillon* (p.14)
12 snails (tinned *au naturel* or freshly cooked)
2 ripe red tomatoes, skinned, deseeded and diced
1 teaspoon tomato purée
1 tablespoon red wine vinegar
6 tablespoons olive oil
juice of half a lemon
a dash of soy sauce
½ teaspoon tarragon, chopped
half a bunch of chives, the tips kept for decoration, the rest snipped
salt, freshly ground pepper

Cooking the crayfish

Wash the crayfish and cook them in the hot *court-bouillon*, allowing 2 minutes' cooking from the moment the liquid comes back to the boil. Remove them and let them cool to lukewarm, then shell the tails, removing the black intestines, and shell the claws. Keep the meat warm, not hot, in a bowl with some of the *court-bouillon*.

Preparing the snails

Rinse the snails under cold running water and drain them well. Cut them into two or three pieces and put them in a bowl. Reserve them.

Making the sauce

Season the diced tomato with salt and pepper and crush it with a wire whisk. Incorporate the vinegar, olive oil, tomato purée, lemon juice, soy sauce and 3 tablespoons of the warm crayfish *court-bouillon*. Lastly, add the snipped herbs. Add the shelled crayfish tails and claws and the snails to the tomato mixture.

Taste for seasoning and divide between four warm bowls or small individual dishes. Arrange the chive tips on top and serve warm.

Hot Terrine of Rascasse with Chive Butter

Terrine chaude de rascasse beurre de ciboulette

For eight or ten people

700g *(1²/₃ lb)* fillets of scorpion fish (rascasse), or gurnard or red mullet
4 egg whites
500ml *(16 fl. oz)* double cream
150g *(5¹/₂ oz)* spinach
250g *(8¹/₂ oz)* raw salmon or shelled scallops, cut into strips

for the chive butter
600g *(1 lb 5 oz)* butter
4 shallots
4 tablespoons white wine vinegar
juice of a lemon
a small bunch of chives
salt, freshly ground pepper, a pinch of cayenne

*Best End of Lamb
with Mushroom Sauce and Courgette Flans.*
(p.124)

Medallions of Crawfish
in a Cream and Curry Sauce
with Red Peppers.
(p.154)

Braised Sweetbreads
Wrapped in Spinach.
(p.166)

Burgundian Duck Foie Gras.
(p.187)

Scallops in their Shells.
(p.195)

Dublin Bay Prawns
with Poached Eggs
and Tarragon Vinegar.
(p.193)

Passion Fruit Mousse.
(p.78)

Grandmother's Orange Gâteau,
Chocolate Tart and
Caramelised Apple Tart.
(pp. 75, 219 and 173)

Making the *farce*

Purée the rascasse fillets by rubbing them through a sieve into a bowl. Add the egg whites one at a time, working each one in with a wooden spatula, then gradually add the cream. Season with salt, pepper and a pinch of cayenne. The mixture should be smooth and supple; reserve it in the refrigerator.

Wash the spinach and cook it in boiling salted water. Refresh under cold running water, press well between the palms of your hands, then purée the spinach and sieve it.

Mix the spinach into one-quarter of the fish *farce*.

Assembling and cooking the terrine

Pre-heat the oven to Reg. 4/350°F/180°C.

Butter a terrine of the appropriate size, line it with greaseproof paper and start with a layer of white fish mixture. Arrange half the strips of salmon or scallops on top. Cover this with another layer of the white mixture, then a layer of spinach mixture. Finish as you began, with a white layer, a layer of salmon or scallops and another white layer.

Smooth the top and cover with a sheet of aluminium foil. Cook for about 1½ hours. Test by plunging a knife into the centre; it is done when the blade comes out clean.

Let it rest for a while and then carefully turn it out on to a board ready to slice.

Making the chive butter

While the terrine is cooking, make a classic *beurre blanc* (p.11) using the quantities given for this recipe. Whisk well and at the last moment add the lemon juice and chives. Taste for seasoning.

Serving the terrine

Arrange a slice of terrine on each of eight or ten plates, using a cake-server to lift the slices. Serve hot or lukewarm, with the chive butter poured over the slices of terrine or handed separately in a sauceboat.

Suggestion

This terrine could also be served cold with a *sauce aigrelette* (p.15).

Medallions of Crawfish in a Cream and Curry Sauce with Red Peppers

Médaillons de langouste à la vapeur aux épices et aux poivrons doux

For four people

1 large crawfish, weighing 600–700g *(1 lb 5 oz–1²⁄₃ lb)*
150g *(5¹⁄₂ oz)* red peppers
4 shallots, chopped
olive oil
200ml *(7 fl. oz)* aromatic white wine *court-bouillon* (p.14)
a pinch of saffron
a pinch of curry powder
200ml *(7 fl. oz)* double cream
25g *(1 oz)* butter
a few sprigs of chervil
salt, freshly ground pepper

Preliminary preparations

Plunge the crawfish into a large pan of boiling salted water and cook for 15–18 minutes.

Pre-heat the oven to Reg. 6/400°F/200°C.

Cook the red peppers in the oven for 12–15 minutes; this will make them easy to peel. Skin them.

When the crawfish is cooked, shell the tail and cut it into even slices (medallions). Turn the oven to its highest setting.

Making the sauce

Sweat the shallots in a very little olive oil until they are tender and translucent. Add the aromatic *court-bouillon* and let it reduce by half. Add the saffron and curry powder and the cream. Reduce again until you have a smooth, shiny sauce that will coat a spoon lightly. Finish the sauce by adding the butter, cut into small pieces. Taste for seasoning.

Finishing and serving the crawfish

Heat the medallions of crawfish by sprinkling them with water and letting them steam in the oven for a few minutes – 2 or 3 minutes should be enough.

Strain the sauce and divide it between four heated soup plates. Arrange the medallions on top.

Decorate with the peppers, cut into strips and interlaced in a herringbone pattern, then sprinkle with a few sprigs of chervil.

Suggestions

The red peppers could be replaced by other vegetables, such as tomatoes cut into dice, asparagus tips or wild mushrooms.

Chicken Liver Flans
with Freshwater Crayfish Sauce

Gâteau de foies blonds aux queues d'écrevisses

For four people

200g *(7 oz)* chicken livers, fresh and as pale as possible
40g *(1 1/2 oz)* flour
3 eggs
3 egg yolks
1 teaspoon meat glaze (optional)
3 tablespoons double cream or *crème fraîche* (p.23)
500ml *(16 fl. oz)* milk
1 small clove of garlic, crushed
500ml *(16 fl. oz)* shellfish sauce (p.17)
1kg *(2 1/4 lb)* freshwater crayfish (cooked as on p.88)
salt, freshly ground pepper, grated nutmeg

Making the chicken liver flans

Remove all the stringy parts and greenish patches from the chicken livers and purée them by working them through a fine sieve. Mix in the flour, and then the eggs, and egg yolks one at a time. Add the meat glaze, cream and milk, and the finely pulverised garlic. Season with salt, pepper and a pinch of nutmeg. Test for flavour by simmering a teaspoonful of the mixture in a small saucepan of water until firm. Adjust the seasoning.

Cooking the flans

Pre-heat the oven to Reg. 2/300°F/150°C.

Transfer the mixture to four or eight individual moulds or one large one, and cook in a bain-marie. The cooking time will vary according to the size of the moulds, but will be about 30 minutes, longer for a single large mould.

Test by inserting the tip of a knife into the centre of one of the moulds. The chicken liver flans are cooked when the blade comes out clean.

155

Serving the chicken liver flans

Heat the shellfish sauce. Shell and heat the freshwater crayfish tails. Turn out the moulds on to four heated plates and coat lightly with the sauce. Arrange the crayfish tails round the flans.

Suggestions

This is a good hot first course. You could try diced lobster or diced sweetbreads in tomato sauce as an alternative garnish.

Chicken à la Crème

Poulet à la crème comme en Bresse

For four people

1 large free-range chicken (a Bresse chicken if possible)
150g *(5½ oz)* butter
1 whole onion, stuck with a clove
1 clove of garlic, peeled
a sprig of thyme
half a bay leaf
2–3 tablespoons flour
500ml *(16 fl. oz)* thick double cream
3 egg yolks
juice of half a lemon
salt, freshly ground pepper

Preparing the chicken

Cut the chicken into eight pieces with a boning knife. First remove the legs and cut them in half to obtain two thighs and two drumsticks. Cut the carcass in half down the middle to divide the two halves of the breast. Detach them from the lower part of the carcass and cut them in half across the middle. Trim off the wing-tips and discard with the carcass and neck.

Cooking the chicken

Melt a generous amount of butter in a large sauté pan and put in the pieces of chicken, well seasoned with salt and pepper. Let them brown gently to a golden colour on all sides.

Add the onion, garlic and herbs, put in a little fresh butter and stir in the flour. Let the flour cook and begin to colour for a moment, then add enough water to cover the pieces of chicken, blending it in with the flour. Stir well and bring to the boil to obtain a smooth sauce, then cover the pan and cook over a moderate heat for about 30 minutes, depending on the size of the chicken.

When the chicken is just done, remove the pieces with a fork and transfer them to another pan.

Finishing the sauce and serving the chicken

Strain the sauce over the pieces of chicken and heat it through. Then add the cream mixed with the egg yolks. Do not boil once this liasion has been added. If the sauce is too thick, add more water or more cream; taste for seasoning and add a squeeze of lemon juice. Serve very hot on a large serving dish.

Suggestions

Serve plain rice or Vonnas pancakes (p.216) with the chicken.

This is a particularly simple recipe. It is interesting that if you use a really top-quality chicken, you don't need to use stock to cook it in. The juices from the chicken, nicely caramelised at the beginning, are what give the sauce its flavours.

Sautéed Scallops with Red Wine and Basil

Sauté de coquilles Saint-Jacques au pinot rouge et au basilic

For four people

24 scallops
200g *(7 oz)* butter
3 shallots, finely chopped
150ml *(5 fl. oz)* red wine
4 very ripe tomatoes, skinned, deseeded and diced
1 teaspoon basil, chopped
2 teaspoons parsley, chopped
2–3 tablespoons double cream
salt, freshly ground pepper

Preparing the scallops

Open the scallops and detach them from their shells with a spoon. Wash them well in cold water and dry them. Cut them in half horizontally if they are very large.

Cooking the scallops

Heat half the butter in a large frying pan and put in the scallops. When they have browned a little, turn them over and carefully brown the other sides. Season well and add the chopped shallot. Let them brown quickly, but not too much. Deglaze with red wine and reduce over a moderate heat.

Add the tomato, basil and parsley and a spoonful of cream. Taste for seasoning and bring the sauce to the right consistency by adding more butter and cream. Serve at once.

Suggestions

The scallops used in this recipe must be very fresh and should not be shelled too far ahead of cooking; their juices will add flavour to the sauce. Take care not to overcook them; you could transfer the scallops to a heated serving dish before you make the sauce.

Roast Partridge with Green Cabbage

Perdreau rôti en cocotte au chou vert

For four people

4 young partridge, freshly shot
4 thin slices of pork fat, for barding
100g *(3¹/₂ oz)* streaky bacon, in a piece, with rind
2 green Savoy cabbages
200g *(7 oz)* butter
1 carrot, coarsely sliced
1 onion, quartered
2 cloves of garlic, peeled
2 shallots, peeled
a sprig of thyme
a bay leaf
100ml *(4 fl. oz)* white wine
a little chicken stock or water
salt, freshly ground pepper

Preliminary preparations

If possible, choose grey partridge, which are a little more tender than the red-legged variety. Truss them and wrap them in the barding fat.

Trim the rind off the bacon. Cut the streaky bacon into little *batons* and blanch with the rind in boiling water to get rid of some of the salt.

Quarter the cabbages, discarding the outside leaves and stalks. Wash and blanch briefly in boiling salted water. Leave in a colander to drain.

Pre-heat the oven to its hottest setting.

Cooking the partridge

Heat 50g *(2 oz)* of the butter in a casserole over a brisk heat. Brown the partridge delicately on all sides and add the carrot, onion, garlic, shallots, herbs and bacon rind.

Add a little more fresh butter and put the casserole, covered, into the hot oven. Cook for 18–20 minutes.

While the partridge are cooking, melt 100g *(4 oz)* butter in a large sauté pan and throw in the little *lardons* of bacon. Allow to brown a little, then add the blanched cabbage, season with salt and pepper, and cook gently, stirring with a wooden spatula. Don't let the cabbage get mushy; it should be just tender and with all its juices evaporated.

Finishing and serving the dish

When the partridge are cooked, keep them hot and make some good gravy in the normal way, pouring off some of the fat from the casserole and deglazing it with a little white wine. Let it reduce and lose its acidity, then add a little water or chicken stock. Reduce again, then strain the gravy, which has taken up all the flavours from the vegetables, herbs and caramelised juices.

Whisk in the rest of the butter, in small pieces, tasting for seasoning. Transfer the cabbage to a large, heated serving dish. Arrange the whole partridge on top or cut them up and place the pieces on top of the cabbage.

Coat generously with the gravy, which will run down into the cabbage, harmonising its flavour with that of the partridge.

Suggestions

Instead of partridge, you could use young pigeons or even young free-range guinea fowl.

Duck with Figs

Canard de Barbarie aux figues

For four people

1 duckling, preferably female, or duck
200g *(7 oz)* butter
1 carrot ⎫
1 leek ⎬ cut into mirepoix dice
1 onion ⎭
8 fresh figs
salt, freshly ground pepper

Cooking the duck

Sweat the mirepoix dice of vegetables in a little butter for several minutes until they are almost tender. Pre-heat the oven to Reg. 9/475°F/240°C.

Melt a nut of butter in an enamelled cast-iron casserole and brown the duckling all over, seasoning it with salt and pepper as it cooks. Then add the mirepoix, cover and cook in the oven for 20 minutes.

Meanwhile cut the figs not quite through into quarters so that they can be opened out like a flower.

Carving the duck

When the duck is cooked, remove the legs and wings, and slice the breasts. Keep hot.

Making the sauce and cooking the figs

Remove the mirepoix from the casserole with a slotted spoon. Deglaze the pan with a little water and put in the figs, cooking them very gently for 5 minutes and then draining them. Purée the mirepoix in a liquidiser or food processor.

Arrange the duck on four heated plates, giving each person a leg or wing and several slices of breast. Arrange two figs beside the duck.

Finish the sauce by adding the mirepoix purée, rubbed through a sieve. Add the remaining butter, cut into pieces, and taste for seasoning. Coat the duck with this sauce and serve very hot.

Suggestions

Serve the duck with fresh pasta tossed in butter.

As this is meant to be a main course, it should be on the generous side, so if the ducks are small allow one between two people (small means less than 1.6kg *(3½ lb)*.

Female ducks have more tender meat; large drakes (weighing up to 2½kg *(5½ lb)*) have firmer flesh and a stronger flavour.

The cooking time will vary according to the size of the duck. Keep the breasts slightly pink; if necessary, the legs can be put back to cook rather longer.

Saddle of Rabbit
with Chayotes and Thyme

Râble de lapin poêlé aux chayotes et au thym

For four people

2 rabbits, each weighing 2kg *(4¹/₂ lb)*
2 tablespoons olive oil
2 carrots, cut into pieces
3 shallots, peeled
1 onion, quartered
2 sprigs of fresh thyme
1 bay leaf
1 clove
800g *(1³/₄ lb)* chayotes (see note)
70g *(2¹/₂ oz)* butter
100ml *(4 fl. oz)* dry white wine
200ml *(7 fl. oz)* chicken stock
1 dessertspoon Dijon mustard
200ml *(7 fl. oz)* double cream or *crème fraîche* (p.23)
salt, freshly ground pepper

Preparing the rabbits

Cut up the rabbits, keeping the two saddles for this recipe. The legs and other pieces can be used to make sautéed rabbit with mustard or with garlic, or jellied rabbit.

Pre-heat the oven to its hottest setting.

Cooking the rabbit

Heat a small roasting tin containing the olive oil. When it is hot, put in the saddles of rabbit and any trimmings, the carrots, shallots and onion, one sprig of thyme, the bay leaf and single clove. Roast in the hot oven for 12–15 minutes. Turn them once or twice during cooking so that they are evenly browned.

Preparing the chayotes

While the rabbit is cooking, cut the chayotes in half and pare them into little pieces the size and shape of a clove of garlic. Cook them in boiling salted water for 10–12 minutes, then drain and fry them very lightly in 35g *(1¹/₂ oz)* of the butter. Keep them hot.

Finishing the rabbit and making the sauce

When they are done, remove the saddles of rabbit to a heated dish and keep them hot while you make the sauce.

162

Skim the fat off the cooking juices, put the roasting tin over a brisk heat and add the white wine.

Reduce, to drive off any acidity, then add the stock. Add the second sprig of thyme, the mustard and cream, stir well and reduce until you have a light, velvety sauce. Taste for seasoning, add the remaining butter, cut in little pieces, and strain.

Serving the saddles

Remove the fillets from the two saddles with a sharp knife, then turn the backbones over and remove the smaller fillets that lie underneath.

Slice the fillets and arrange them in the middle of four heated plates. Arrange the chayotes round the edge and coat everything with the sauce. Serve at once.

Suggestions

Choose plump domestic rabbits; if you prefer, you can cook the saddles with the hind legs intact.

The saddles could be marinated with the vegetables, herbs and clove for 24 hours in the refrigerator (prevent it from becoming dry by coating everything with a little olive oil); this will make it even more tender and deliciously flavoured.

When possible, use fresh thyme to flavour the sauce.

Note

Chayotes resemble a pale-green avocado in appearance and have a large central pip. In texture they are rather like very firm courgettes. They are available in season from good greengrocers and supermarkets.

Farmed Pigeons
with Grapes and Red Wine Sauce

Pigeonneau de Bresse aux raisins sauce vigneronne

4 plump pigeons
32 grapes (seedless if possible), peeled
1 bottle red wine, strong, deep in colour and low in acidity
1 carrot, coarsely sliced
1 onion, cut into quarters
a sprig of thyme
1 bay leaf
150g *(5½ oz)* butter
1 teaspoon *beurre manié*
1 teaspoon shallot, chopped
1 teaspoon tarragon, chopped
1 teaspoon parsley or chervil, chopped
croûtons for garnishing
salt, freshly ground pepper

Cooking the pigeons

Pre-heat the oven to its hottest setting.

Put the pigeons in an enamelled iron casserole with the carrot, onion, herbs and 30g *(1 oz)* of the butter. Brown the pigeons a little on top of the stove, then season, cover the casserole and cook in the oven for 15–20 minutes, turning and basting them several times.

Making the sauce

When the pigeons are done, take them out of the oven, cover them with aluminium foil and keep them hot.

Skim off most of the fat from the casserole and pour in the red wine. Heat it, flame it and let it reduce by half, adding the *beurre manié* in small pieces and whisking it in.

The sauce will thicken very slightly; it should coat the spoon, but very lightly. Taste for seasoning, and add the tarragon and chopped shallot. Let it boil for an instant, whisking vigorously to infuse the flavours.

Strain the sauce into a saucepan and finish it by adding 60g *(2 oz)* of the butter, cut into small pieces (or a little cream, or a little of each).

Finishing and serving the pigeons

Sauté the peeled grapes briefly in the remaining 60g *(2 oz)* of butter. Cut them in half first if they are large, and remove any pips.

164

Arrange the pigeons, whole or, better still, carved into pieces with the carcasses removed, on a large serving dish. Put the grapes round the outside. Coat everything with the red wine sauce and sprinkle with chopped parsley or chervil. Arrange *croûtons* here and there, and serve at once.

Stew of Freshwater Fish '*Comme aux Bords de Saône*'

Pochouse comme aux bords de Saône

For five or six people

1–2 eels *(800g-1kg/1³⁄₄–2¹⁄₄ lb)*, skinned
3 burbot
1 carp *(800g-1kg/1³⁄₄–2¹⁄₄ lb)*
1 pike or zander
1 perch or other river fish
2 white onions, sliced
200g *(7 oz)* carrots, sliced
200g *(7 oz)* butter
1 *bouquet garni*
3 cloves of garlic, crushed
1 litre *(1³⁄₄ pints)* white wine
150g *(5¹⁄₂ oz)* lean streaky bacon, cut into lardons
beurre manié made with 40g *(1¹⁄₂ oz)* flour
50ml *(2 fl. oz)* cream
juice of a lemon or a dash of vinegar
croûtons, to garnish the stew
1 tablespoon parsley, chopped
salt, freshly ground pepper

Preparing the fish

Have all the fish cleaned, trimmed and scaled. Cut them into pieces 8–10cm *(3–4 in)* long.

Making the stew

Soften the onions and carrots in a large pan in 100g *(3¹⁄₂ oz)* butter. Add the slices of fish, *bouquet garni*, garlic and salt and pepper. Pour in the white wine and cook gently for 20–25 minutes. Keep an eye on the cooking and lift out the pieces of fish as they are done.

Meanwhile, blanch the lardons of bacon in boiling water, then fry them gently in butter in a large sauté pan.

Arrange the pieces of fish in the pan with the bacon and keep them hot.

Making the sauce and serving the fish stew

Finish the sauce by whisking the *beurre manié*, broken into little pieces, into the fish cooking juices. Whisk in the cream and the remaining butter, cut into pieces. Season and add a dash of lemon juice or vinegar.

Strain this sauce over the fish, then decorate with *croûtons* and chopped parsley. Serve very hot.

Suggestions

You could add little glazed onions or spring onions stewed in butter to the sauce, and possibly steamed potatoes.

Braised Sweetbreads Wrapped in Spinach

Paupiette de ris de veau braisé

For four people

600g *(1 lb 5 oz)* veal sweetbreads (2–3 sweetbreads)
500g *(1 lb 2 oz)* onion, carrot, leek, shallot and garlic, coarsely
  chopped
80g *(3 oz)* butter
bouquet garni of 1 sprig thyme, 1 bay leaf and 1 clove
50ml *(2 fl. oz)* dry white wine
1 litre *(1¾ pints)* clarified stock
2 teaspoons *beurre manié*
a pinch of curry powder
1 teaspoon Dijon mustard
500ml *(16 fl. oz)* double cream or *crème fraîche* (p.23)
100g *(3½ oz)* spinach
salt, freshly ground pepper

Preliminary preparations

Prick the sweetbreads with a trussing needle and soak them in cold water for at least an hour. Then bring them to the boil in salted water and let them cook for 3 minutes. Remove them, refresh them under cold running water and pare away the tough outer skin and membrane.

Wash the spinach, remove the stalks and blanch it in boiling salted water for a few seconds.

Cooking the sweetbreads

Sweat the chopped vegetables and herbs in a little of the butter in a heavy pan or casserole. Place the sweetbreads on top, pour in the wine, season and add enough stock almost to cover the sweetbreads. Cover the pan and simmer for 15 minutes. Remove the sweetbreads and keep them hot, without refreshing them.

Making the sauce

Reduce the sweetbread cooking liquid by half, whisk in a little *beurre manié* broken into pieces, and add the curry powder and a very little mustard. Stir in the cream and reduce again until the sauce will coat a spoon.

Wrapping up and serving the sweetbreads

Meanwhile, cut each sweetbread into pieces the size of a normal *paupiette*. Roll each one in a spinach leaf or two and keep them hot in a deep serving dish. Allow two *paupiettes* to each person.

Taste the sauce for seasoning; it should be a beautiful, pale, straw-gold colour. Strain it through a fine sieve and whisk in the remaining butter, cut into pieces, at the last minute. Pour it over the sweetbreads and serve at once.

Suggestions

If the sweetbreads are prepared ahead of time, keep them hot in an air-tight container, with a bit of stock in the bottom.

This is an exquisite way of serving sweetbreads, either as a first or main course, depending on the rest of the menu.

You could enhance the presentation by arranging little bouquets of fresh tomato dice in the sauce round the sides of the sweetbreads.

167

Rabbit Pilaf with Paprika

Pilaf de lapin au paprika

For four or six people

1 rabbit, weighing 2kg *(4¹/₂ lb)*, cut into pieces
2 carrots ⎫
2 onions ⎭ cut into large mirepoix dice
2 cloves of garlic, crushed
1 *bouquet garni*
300g *(10¹/₂ oz)* butter
1 tablespoon flour
100ml *(4 fl. oz)* dry white wine
2 tablespoons paprika
half an onion, finely chopped
400g *(14 oz)* long-grain rice
2 litres *(3¹/₂ pints)* chicken stock or water
3 tablespoons double cream
salt, freshly ground pepper

Cooking the rabbit

Heat 100g *(3¹/₂ oz)* butter in a sauté pan and brown the pieces of rabbit all over. Stir in the flour and the diced vegetables, garlic and herbs. Sweat over a moderate heat until the flour has turned a good golden colour, adding more butter if necessary.

Deglaze with the white wine, add the paprika and add enough stock or water almost to cover the rabbit. Season and simmer for 1–1½ hours, keeping an eye on the cooking.

Preparing the rice

Melt 100g *(3¹/₂ oz)* butter in a deep sauté pan and sweat the onion without letting it brown. Pour in the rice, stir it round and then add about 1½ times its volume of chicken stock. Cook it, preferably in the oven at Reg. 6/400°F/200°C, for about 20 minutes, adding more stock if necessary. Stir it up with a fork, adding a lump of butter, when it is just cooked.

Finishing and serving the rabbit

Remove the pieces of rabbit with a slotted spoon when they are done, and keep them hot in a serving dish.

Reduce the sauce until it is smooth and velvety, add the cream and, if necessary, add a little more paprika to heighten the taste.

Whisk in the remaining butter, cut into small pieces, and strain the sauce over the rabbit.

168

Serve with the rice on the same dish, generously covered with sauce.

Suggestions

Instead of using chicken stock, you could use the rabbit trimmings to give flavour to the dish. Strain them out with the vegetables just before serving.

You could add diced tomato or diced cooked red peppers to the sauce at the last moment. Cook the peppers in the oven for 20 minutes at Reg. 6/400°F/200°C with a little olive oil.

Stuffed Pigeons with Wild Mushroom Sauce

Pigeon de Bresse farci crème forestière

For four people

2 large or 4 smaller domesticated pigeons, with their livers and
    hearts
100g *(3½ oz)* purée of *foie gras*
30g *(1 oz)* plain ham
1 small teaspoon Dijon mustard
300g *(10½ oz)* wild mushrooms (ceps, chanterelles or morels)
150g *(5½ oz)* butter
1 shallot, chopped
6 tablespoons double cream
a dash of vinegar
1 carrot, sliced
1 onion, sliced
2 cloves of garlic
half a glass of dry white wine
salt, freshly ground pepper

Boning and stuffing the pigeons

Bone the pigeons, starting by cutting them open along the back so that the breast bones can be removed from inside. Leave the leg and wing bones in place. Keep the hearts and livers for the *farce*. Reserve the carcasses.

Put the hearts, livers, *foie gras* and ham into a food processor and reduce to a purée. Add a teaspoon of mustard and season the mixture with salt and pepper.

169

Spread the *farce* over the inside of the pigeons and close them up, sewing them with trussing string and keeping them as near as possible to their original shape.

Preparing the mushroom sauce

Clean and wash the mushrooms and blanch them in boiling salted water for a few minutes. Chop them coarsely and sweat them in a little butter with the shallot, without letting them brown. Add the cream and let it simmer, but do not reduce too much. Season with salt, pepper and a dash of vinegar.

Pre-heat the oven to Reg. 5/375°F/190°C.

Cooking the pigeons

Put the pigeons in a casserole with a generous quantity of butter, the carrot, onion, garlic and the pigeon carcasses. Cook, covered, for 30 minutes, turning the pigeons frequently. Skim off the fat, add the white wine and return the pan to the oven for about 5 minutes. Then remove the pigeons and keep them hot.

Making the gravy and serving the pigeons

Add a little water to the cooking juices, simmer, season and strain the gravy into a small pan. Finish by whisking in the rest of the butter, cut into small pieces.

If they are large, cut the pigeons in half. Cover the bottom of four heated plates with the hot mushroom sauce, place the pigeons on top and coat lightly with the gravy.

Suggestions

The *farce* could be enriched with port or brandy and chopped truffles.

The gravy made from the cooking juices should be fairly strong to enhance the flavour of the mushroom sauce.

Pheasant with Sauerkraut

Faisan à la choucroute

For four people

1 pheasant
1½kg *(3½ lb)* sauerkraut
400g *(14 oz)* salt belly of pork

for the sauerkraut

150g *(5½ oz)* goose or duck fat
a few strips of salt pork rind
2 carrots, cut into pieces
1 onion, stuck with 2 cloves
1 clove of garlic
thyme, a bay leaf
4–5 juniper berries
half a glass dry white Alsace wine
750ml *(27 fl. oz)* clear chicken stock or water

for the pheasant

1 carrot
1 onion, cut in half
1 clove of garlic
butter
salt, freshly ground pepper

Preparing the sauerkraut

Rinse and drain the sauerkraut. Melt half the goose fat in a large casserole over a brisk heat, add the strips of pork rind, the salt pork, the sauerkraut, vegetables, herbs, spices and wine and 500ml *(16 fl. oz)* of chicken stock. Season lightly with salt and pepper, bring to the boil and simmer for 1½ hours, stirring occasionally with a wooden spatula. Test the sauerkraut from time to time; it should still have a bit of bite to it.

Cooking the pheasant

Pre-heat the oven to its highest setting.

Truss the pheasant and brown it all over with some of the goose fat in a casserole in the hot oven. Add the carrot, onion and garlic, cover the casserole and cook for about 30–40 minutes, according to the size of the bird, basting and turning it frequently.

Finishing and serving the pheasant

When the pheasant is cooked, remove it from the casserole and keep it hot. Make some good gravy, deglazing the casserole with the remaining stock or water. Allow to reduce by half, strain through a fine wire sieve into a small saucepan and whisk in some butter, cut into small pieces, to give the gravy a velvety texture.

Arrange the sauerkraut in a large heated serving dish. Cut up the pheasant and place the pieces on top.

Moisten the pheasant with the gravy and arrange a border of thinly sliced salt pork round the edge to complete this savoury, country dish.

Fig Compote
with Orange and Lemon Juice

Compote de figues au jus d'agrumes

For eight people

16 handsome figs, green or purple
500ml *(16 fl. oz)* fresh orange juice
250ml *(8 fl. oz)* lemon juice
500g *(1 lb 2 oz)* caster sugar
a few mint leaves

Carefully peel the figs, keeping them whole.

Prepare a syrup of the orange and lemon juices and the sugar in a stainless-steel or enamelled saucepan. Melt the sugar, stirring, then bring to the boil, remove the pan from the heat and put in the figs. Allow to cool and serve very cold, decorated with a few mint leaves.

Caramelised Apple Tart

Tarte aux pommes caramélisées

For four people

4 good apples (not too hard)
250g *(8½ oz)* shortcrust pastry (see below)
100g *(3½ oz)* butter, softened
150g *(5½ oz)* caster sugar

for the shortcrust pastry

150g *(5½ oz)* flour
90g *(3½ oz)* butter
a pinch of salt
50ml *(2 fl. oz)* water

Preparing the pastry

Make the shortcrust pastry in the normal way and let it rest for half an hour. Roll it out 2mm *(⅛ in)* thick and use it to line a buttered tart ring placed on a buttered baking sheet. Prick the pastry with a fork.

173

Preparing the apple tart

Pre-heat the oven to Reg. 7/425°F/220°C.

Peel, halve and core the apples, then cut them into slices the thickness of a matchstick.

Sprinkle the bottom of the pastry case lightly with sugar and dot it with little pieces of butter, then arrange the slices of apple, overlapping, on top.

Brush generously with butter and sprinkle plenty of sugar over the top.

Cooking the apple tart

Bake for about 20 minutes, adding more sugar and butter while cooking if necessary, to obtain a well-caramelised finish to the apples. Serve warm.

Fresh Peach Sorbet

Sorbet à la pêche de vigne

For four people

1.2kg *(2 lb 10 oz)* fresh peaches, very red, ripe and juicy
juice of half a lemon
500ml *(16 fl. oz)* water
500g *(1 lb 2 oz)* sugar

Make a syrup by dissolving the sugar in the water and bringing it to the boil. Allow to cool.

Skin the peaches and remove the stones. Purée them in a *mouli-légumes* placed over a mixing bowl, using the fine blade. Add the lemon juice and the cooled syrup. Freeze in a sorbet-maker, having added more syrup or lemon juice if necessary.

Suggestions

Avoid using peaches with a floury texture for this sorbet. You can also make lovely sorbets with white peaches; the results always depend on the rich flavour and juiciness of the fruit.

Serve in a glass, with a dash of *crème de cassis* or strawberry *eau-de-vie* poured over the top.

Almond Tuiles

Tuiles aux amandes

For eight people

250g *(8¹/₂ oz)* slivered almonds
250g *(8¹/₂ oz)* caster sugar
75g *(2¹/₂ oz)* flour, sieved
4 egg whites
1 whole egg
25g *(1 oz)* melted butter

Making the biscuit mixture

Put the almonds, sugar and sieved flour into a large bowl and mix them together thoroughly. Add the egg whites and whole egg, stirring carefully so that the almonds do not break. Pour in the melted butter and mix thoroughly.

Pre-heat the oven to Reg. 4/350°F/180°C.

Cooking the *tuiles*

Brush a baking sheet with melted butter and put teaspoons of the mixture, well spaced out, on the baking sheet. Flatten each one into a round with the back of a fork dipped in cold water. Bake for about 10 minutes.

As soon as you remove them from the oven, roll each *tuile* round a rolling pin, or use a special curved baking sheet made for the purpose.

Suggestion

Eat at once or as soon as possible. If not, *tuiles* must be stored in an air-tight container.

Chestnut Soufflé Cake

Gâteau soufflé aux châtaignes

For four people

1¹/₂kg *(3¹/₂ lb)* chestnuts
1.2kg *(2 lb 10 oz)* sugar
1 vanilla pod
200g *(7 oz)* butter
8 eggs, separated
softened butter for the cake tin

Making the cake mixture

Melt 1kg *(2¼ lb)* of the sugar in 1 litre *(1¾ pints)* of water together with the vanilla pod, then bring to the boil.

Make a slit in the rounded side of each chestnut with a small, sharp knife. Blanch them for 5–6 minutes in a large pan of boiling water, drain and refresh them, then remove the shells and inner skin. Cook them in the syrup for 10–15 minutes until tender.

Pre-heat the oven to Reg. 4/350°F/180°C.

Purée the chestnuts and press the purée through a fine sieve. Add the butter, 200g *(7 oz)* sugar and the egg yolks.

Butter a cake tin of the appropriate size.

At the last moment whisk the egg whites to a snow and fold them delicately into the chestnut mixture.

Cooking the cake

Transfer the mixture to the buttered cake tin and cook in a bain-marie for 30 minutes. Test by inserting a trussing needle into the centre of the cake. Allow the cake to cool in its tin, then turn it out and serve chilled.

Suggestions

Serve the chestnut soufflé cake with chocolate sauce, and decorate it with a border of *marrons glacés*.

Prunes in Red Wine and Marc du Bugey

Pruneaux au vin rouge at au marc du Bugey

For eight people

1.2kg *(2 lb 10 oz)* large prunes (preferably *pruneaux d'Agen*)
1 litre *(1¾ pints)* strong red wine
1kg *(2¼ lb)* granulated sugar
zest and juice of 1 orange
zest and juice of 1 lemon
200ml *(7 fl. oz)* Marc du Bugey or other marc
1 vanilla pod
5g *(large pinch)* ground cinnamon
a pot of freshly made tea for one

Prepare one or two days in advance.

Preliminary preparations

Soak the prunes for about 1 hour and drain them thoroughly.

Bring the red wine to the boil and flame it. When the flames die down, melt the sugar in the wine and add the orange and lemon zests and juice, vanilla pod, cinnamon and tea.

Cooking the prunes

Put the prunes in the red wine syrup, bring it back to the boil and cook them at a rolling boil for 5 minutes. Remove the pan from the heat and allow to cool. Then add the marc and leave to macerate for a day or two in a cool place before serving.

Suggestions

Serve with a slice of brioche, as you would a cooked compote of fruit. For this recipe you can use rum or fruit eau-de-vie instead of marc.

Quince Paste

Pâte de coings

1kg *(2¼ lb)* quinces
800g *(1¾ lb)* sugar
zest and juice of 1 lemon
zest and juice of 1 orange
granulated sugar

Peel the quinces and grate them coarsely. Weigh the pulp.

Cook the pulp with an equal weight of sugar, and the grated orange and lemon zests and juice. Cook until you have a dryish purée, stirring constantly.

When the mixture becomes translucent, pour it into a buttered rectangular Swiss roll tin and leave to cool. Cut into even pieces, any size you like, and roll the pieces in granulated sugar.

Leave to dry on a rack, and keep in an air-tight container in a dry place.

Chocolate Truffles

Truffes au chocolat

1 litre *(1¾ pints)* double cream
1.3kg *(2 lb 12 oz)* dark chocolate
500g *(1 lb 2 oz) couverture* or bitter cooking chocolate
150g *(5½ oz)* unsweetened cocoa powder

Heat the cream to boiling point.

Melt the dark chocolate in a saucepan over a bain-marie. Remove it from the heat, pour on the boiling cream and mix until you have a smooth mixture. Chill in the refrigerator for 2–3 hours to stiffen the mixture.

Melt the *couverture* or bitter chocolate in a saucepan over a bain-marie.

Remove the chocolate mixture from the refrigerator and roll into little truffle-sized balls, using a teaspoon to scoop out small quantities and rolling them between your palms or using a potato-baller.

Dip the truffles into the barely warm *couverture* or cooking chocolate and then roll them in the cocoa powder. Let them harden a little in a cold place before enjoying them.

Suggestions

To keep these truffles, put them somewhere cold, or in the lower part of the refrigerator, preferably in an air-tight container to avoid humidity. They will keep for about 10 days.

Winter

Salade Jacqueline

For four people

4 good handfuls of various winter salad leaves, whatever is in
    season (lamb's lettuce, escarole, frizzy endive, chicory, etc.)
4 artichokes
half a lemon
cooked 'oysters' from 4–5 chickens or 2 poached chicken breasts
    (see p.28)
4 slices of prosciutto or good quality cooked ham
classic vinaigrette (p.37)
1 fresh truffle, cut into julienne strips
1 hard-boiled egg, chopped
salt, freshly ground pepper

Preliminary preparations

Wash all the salad stuff and dry it well. Set aside, wrapped in a teatowel.

Wash the artichokes and break off the stalks. Cut the tops off with a sharp knife. Trim the leaves away from the bases, making a circular cutting arc with a sharp knife. Remove all the tough, non-edible parts, leaving only the hearts. Rub with half a lemon.

Cooking the artichoke hearts

Cook the hearts in boiling salted water, uncovered, for 20 minutes. Test by piercing with a sharp knife or trussing needle. Refresh under cold running water. Remove the spiny chokes carefully with a spoon.

Preparing the chicken and ham

If using 'oysters', cut them in half; if chicken breasts, cut them into large dice. Cut the ham into large julienne strips.

Finishing the salad

Just before serving the salad, put the leaves in a large salad bowl, add a few pinches of salt and toss the salad with the vinaigrette. Divide between four large plates.

Put a little more vinaigrette into the salad bowl and toss the artichoke hearts in it. Put them on top of the salads and fill them with strips of ham and chopped hard-boiled egg, with the truffles on top. Arrange the pieces of chicken round the sides, having first dipped them into the vinaigrette.

Suggestions

If you want a richer version, replace the ham with *foie gras* in a slice, in which case you will not need the chicken.

Poultry Liver Mousse with Truffles

Mousse de foies de volaille truffée

For four people

250–300g *(8¹/₂–10¹/₂ oz)* chicken or duck livers, or a mixture of
   the two
20g *(³/₄ oz)* butter
1 tablespoon brandy
1 tablespoon port
150g *(5¹/₂ oz)* goose or duck *foie gras* or purée of *foie gras*
150ml *(¹/₄ pint)* double cream or *crème fraîche* (p.23)
20g *(³/₄ oz)* chopped truffles
250ml *(8 fl. oz)* strong jellied chicken stock (half for the mousse
   and half for the decoration)
salt, freshly ground pepper

Make 24 hours in advance.

Preparing the livers

Trim the livers, removing all the strings and fibres. Sauté them briefly in a little butter without letting them brown too much or become dry. Season with salt and pepper and transfer them to a liquidiser or food processor.

Deglaze the pan with the brandy and port, strain the liquid on to the livers and purée them, adding first the *foie gras*, then the cream and half the melted chicken jelly.

When you have a smooth mixture, press it through a fine sieve. Taste for seasoning and add the chopped truffles.

Finishing the mousse

Transfer the mixture to a terrine and let it chill, then pour the remaining jelly over the top. Chill in the refrigerator for at least 24 hours before serving. Serve with toast, preferably made from coarse, sour-dough bread (*pain de campagne*).

Suggestions

You could add skinned pistachio nuts instead of truffles.

To make the presentation more unusual, roll the mixture into balls the size of truffles, adding more *foie gras* to the livers. Set them in the coldest part of the refrigerator and serve them rolled in chopped truffles. They could be served as an accompaniment to a fillet of beef in jelly.

Hot Scallops in Cold Hazelnut Sauce

Chaud-froid de coquilles Saint-Jacques à l'huile de noisette

For four people

12–16 scallops (3 or 4 per person, according to size)
250ml *(8 fl. oz)* home-made mayonnaise (made with olive oil and
    a dash of hazelnut oil)
1 teaspoon green herb mustard
3 tablespoons aromatic white wine *court-bouillon* (p.14)
a dash of white wine vinegar
juice of half a lemon
2 tablespoons chives, snipped
20g *(¾ oz)* butter
sea salt, freshly ground pepper

Making the mayonnaise sauce

Put the mayonnaise into a salad bowl, add the mustard and make the mixture
liquid enough to coat the back of a spoon by adding a little *court-bouillon*,
white wine vinegar and lemon juice. Taste for seasoning, add the chives, and
reserve.

Cooking the scallops

Shell the scallops, remove the beards and coral, and wash them to remove
every trace of sand. Heat the grill or the oven to its highest setting.

Slice the scallops horizontally into two or three slices and spread them out on
four lightly buttered plates. Season lightly with coarse salt and pepper.

Place straight under the grill or in the top of the oven. They will take about 2
minutes to cook.

Remove from the heat and coat with the sauce, using a spoon. Serve at once.

Suggestions

Hazelnut oil has a very pervasive flavour. When you are making the sauce,
take care not to let it dominate the other flavours.

Jellied Terrine of Duck

Terrine campagnarde de canard en gelée

For about fifteen people

1–2 large ducks, weighing 2½–3kg *(5½–6½ lb)* altogether
300g *(10½ oz)* shoulder or tenderloin of pork
300g *(10½ oz)* lean veal
400g *(14 oz)* fat streaky bacon
a pinch of *quatre épices* (p.58)
2–3 tablespoons truffle juice (optional)
a dash of brandy
100ml *(4 fl. oz)* port
200g *(7 oz)* mirepoix dice of carrot, onion and shallot
100g *(3½ oz)* butter
1 litre *(1¾ pints)* strong jellied poultry stock
10 chicken livers, trimmed
100g *(3½ oz) foie gras* or purée of *foie gras*
1–2 truffles, coarsely chopped
sheets of beaten pork back-fat for barding
salt, freshly ground pepper

Make 2–3 days in advance.

Preliminary preparations

If possible, use one very large duck, which will have more flavour than the smaller ones.

Bone the duck and cut the flesh into strips about ½cm *(¼ in)* thick. Cut the pork, veal and bacon into strips of the same size and put them all into a salad bowl. Season with salt, pepper and *quatre épices*, add the truffle juice, brandy and port, and marinate for at least half a day in a cold place.

Making the stock

Cut the duck carcass and neck into pieces and sauté them in a little butter with the vegetable mirepoix, then add a little water. Simmer until well reduced, sieve and add the jellied stock.

Cooking the livers

Sauté the duck's liver and the chicken livers in butter, seasoning them with salt and pepper. Keep an eye on the cooking, turning down the heat so that the livers stay pink inside and do not dry out.

Assembling and cooking the terrine

Pre-heat the oven to Reg. 4/350°F/180°C.

Mince or chop the marinated meats medium fine, except for the fillets of duck breast, which are kept whole. Mince the chicken livers and *foie gras* and work them into the minced meats. Add the marinade and chopped truffles.

Line the bottom and sides of a terrine 28–30cm *(11–12 in)* long and 10cm *(4 in)* deep with the sheets of pork back-fat. Fill with the meat, laying in the strips of duck lengthwise here and there. Stand it in a bain-marie and cover the top with greaseproof paper. Cook in the moderate oven for 2 hours.

Finishing the terrine

When the terrine is ready, press it with a weighted board (not too heavy) as it cools. After 2 hours, bring the liquid jelly and duck stock to the boil and boil for 10 minutes. Skim well, removing all the fat from the top, and then pour, a little at a time, into the warm terrine so that it is absorbed into the meat.

Chill for 2–3 days and serve, preferably not too cold so that you obtain the full flavour.

Suggestions

The duck-stock jelly, which gives a luscious texture to the terrine, is essential and should be very well flavoured.

Keep the oven temperature moderate and do not press for too long as the terrine cools.

The terrine can be accompanied by various small salads according to your own ideas.

My Own Gourmet's Surprise

Amuse-gourmand à ma façon

For four people

1kg *(2¼ lb)* freshwater crayfish
1 lobster, weighing 600–700g *(1 lb 5 oz–1⅔ lb)*
8 very thin slices of salmon (like slices of ham)
60g *(2 oz)* Beluga caviare
100ml *(4 fl. oz)* olive oil
100ml *(4 fl. oz)* lemon juice
1 tablespoon chives, chopped
a handful of very fine French beans, cooked
1 tablespoon vinaigrette
1 tablespoon white wine vinegar
half a lemon, cut into thin slices
4 good lettuce leaves, cut into strips
4 tablespoons mayonnaise
juice of half a lemon
1 teaspoon green herb mustard
salt, freshly ground pepper

Preliminary preparations

Soak the crayfish in a large basin of cold water.

Cook the lobster in boiling salted water, allowing 15 minutes from the time the water returns to the boil. Take it out and refresh it in cold water.

Throw the crayfish into the simmering water, leave them for 2 minutes, then remove the pan from the heat and allow them to cool in their cooking liquid.

Shell the lobster tail and claws carefully. Cut the tail into eight slices and cut the claws in half lengthwise.

Shell the crayfish, removing the black intestines by making an incision along their backs with a sharp knife.

Reserve the lobster on a plate and the crayfish separately in a bowl.

Marinating the salmon

Shortly before you are ready to serve the dish, prepare a marinade by mixing the olive oil and lemon juice, half and half, in a flat bowl. Season it and marinate the slices of salmon for 3 minutes, then drain them. Sprinkle on both sides with chopped chives and then roll up the slices like thin cigars.

Finishing and serving the shellfish and salmon

In the centre of each of four plates put a little bouquet of beans dressed with vinaigrette. Arrange the salmon around the sides, decorated with thin slices of lemon. On one side arrange the lettuce, cut into strips, with a little salad of crayfish tails mixed with half the mayonnaise, which should be made a little thinner with lemon juice. Put the lobster beside the crayfish, two medallions and half a claw each, coated with the rest of the mayonnaise flavoured with green herb mustard. Lastly, decorate with a spoonful of caviare.

Suggestions

This cold first course is expensive but easy to do. You can vary it according to your pocket and your own taste. Make sure it looks as beautiful as possible.

Burgundian Duck Foie Gras

Foie gras de canard à la bourguignonne

For eight people

8 generous slices of duck *foie gras*, weighing 700g *(1²/₃ lb)* altogether
100g *(3¹/₂ oz)* butter

for the jelly

200g *(7 oz)* shallots, chopped
500g *(1 lb 2 oz)* lean beef, cut into cubes
3 cloves of garlic, crushed
1 veal bone
half a leek
2 carrots
1 tomato, coarsely chopped
2 cloves
a sprig of thyme
1 bay leaf

1 litre *(1³/₄ pints)* strong, well-rounded red wine
small glass of *crème de cassis*
1 litre *(1³/₄ pints)* strong, well-flavoured jellied stock
salt, freshly ground pepper

187

Preparing the jelly

Melt the butter in a large pan and put in all the flavourings for the jelly. Let them brown very lightly. Meanwhile, bring the wine to the boil and flame it, then pour it over the contents of the pan. Season with salt and pepper and add the *cassis* and the jellied stock.

Bring back to the boil and reduce very gently, skimming well, to one-quarter of its volume. Allow to cool, then test the jelly on a plate. If it will not set, add a little gelatine.

Coating and serving the *foie gras*

You can use home-made *foie gras* for this recipe.

Put the slices of *foie gras* on a rack and chill them in the refrigerator. Then coat each slice with the jelly, giving them several successive coats and using a spoon to cover them with the jelly. When they are all well covered, trim the edges neatly with a knife. Keep covered in the refrigerator until ready to serve (not too long).

Serve with toasted sour-dough bread (*pain de campagne*).

Suggestion

You can make this jelly with strong duck stock if you happen to have the necessary ingredients.

Fresh Pasta with Oranges and Lemons

Pâtes fraîches aux agrumes

For four people

for the pasta
215g *(7½ oz)* flour
1 teaspoon olive oil
1 egg
1 egg white
1 small teaspoon salt
a little water

1 lemon (unsprayed if possible)
2 oranges (unsprayed if possible)
100ml *(4 fl. oz)* dry white wine
200ml *(4 fl. oz)* double cream or *crème fraîche* (p.23)
grated Parmesan cheese
salt, freshly ground pepper

Making the pasta

Make the pasta by mixing all the ingredients together in a bowl. Knead well into a dough and leave to rest for at least 1 hour in a cool place.

Roll out as finely as possible on a lightly floured table and cut into thin, even ribbons.

Making the sauce

Wash, dry and grate the orange and lemon zests. Put the grated zest in a sauté pan with the white wine and reduce by half. Keep hot.

Cooking and serving the pasta

Bring a large pan of salted water to the boil and cook the pasta for about 5 minutes. Drain and put into the pan with the lemon and orange zests, then add the cream.

Let the pasta absorb the cream, adding more cream if necessary. Taste for seasoning and stir in the grated Parmesan cheese. Serve at once.

Suggestions

Cook the pasta just before you want to serve it, and take care not to overcook it.

You could add a dash of lemon juice to the sauce to underline the citrus flavour.

189

Pumpkin Gratin

Gratin de courge

For six people

half a medium pumpkin, ripe and heavily scented
1 *bouquet garni*
5 cloves of garlic
double cream
75g *(2¹/₂ oz)* Gruyère cheese, finely grated
salt, pepper, nutmeg and cayenne

Cooking the pumpkin

Peel the pumpkin, remove the seeds and cut it into even slices. Put them in a saucepan of boiling salted water with the *bouquet garni* and 3 cloves of garlic. After about 12 minutes, when the pumpkin is nearly cooked (the flesh can be easily crushed with a fork), lift out the pieces with a slotted spoon or skimmer and put them to drain on a cloth so that they lose all their excess moisture.

Finishing and serving the *gratin*

Rub one or possibly two large *gratin* dishes with garlic, and arrange the pieces of pumpkin in the bottom. Crush them coarsely with a fork. Season with salt and pepper, add a little grated nutmeg and cayenne, and pour in enough cream to cover the pumpkin.

Heat the oven to Reg. 6/400°F/200°C.

Sprinkle the *gratin* with finely grated Gruyère and bake until the *gratin* is golden and luscious, with a delicious smell.

Suggestions

You could equally well make this recipe with courgettes. Make sure, in either case, that the vegetables are very well drained – cook them the day before if possible.

Sea-bream with Preserved Lemons

Daurade aux citrons confits

For four people

1 large sea-bream, weighing 1½–2kg *(3½–4½ lb)*
4 preserved lemons (see below)
sprigs of thyme
2 bay leaves
3 tablespoons olive oil
6 tablespoons dry white wine
salt, freshly ground pepper

for the lemons
4 lemons (unsprayed if possible)
coarse salt
1 tablespoon coriander seeds
1 teaspoon black peppercorns
1 dozen cloves

Making the preserved lemons (at least one month ahead)

Wash and dry the lemons, cut them into quarters vertically, without cutting right through, so that they are joined at the bottom. Sprinkle the cut surfaces with coarse salt and put the lemons back in their original shape.

Put them in a jar with the spices and cover with water brought to the boil and then cooled to lukewarm. Seal hermetically and preserve in a cold place for at least a month.

Cooking the sea-bream

Pre-heat the oven to Reg. 4–5/350–375°F/180–190°C.

Clean and scale the fish or ask the fishmonger to do it for you. Put it in a *gratin* dish with the thyme, bay leaves and a little olive oil. Add the white wine, season and cook in the oven for about 10 minutes, basting with the juices in the dish.

Place the preserved lemons round the fish and cook for a further 15 minutes.

Serve by removing the bream fillets in four long pieces and arranging them on four heated plates. Serve with the lemons by the side and the cooking juices poured over the top.

Suggestion

You could serve plain boiled rice with this dish.

191

Stuffed Squid with Wild Rice

Encornets farcis au riz sauvage

For four people

8 squid
5 onions
2 cloves of garlic
150g *(5¹/₂ oz)* green streaky bacon
3 tablespoons parsley, chopped
6 tablespoons olive oil
225g *(8 oz)* wild rice
a strip of orange zest
1 tablespoon brandy
350ml *(12 fl. oz)* dry white wine
1 *bouquet garni*
1 teaspoon thyme leaves
1 tablespoon tomato purée
1 fresh chilli pepper
1 egg yolk
extra chopped parsley
salt, freshly ground pepper

Stuffing the squid

Clean the squid without splitting them, remove the insides and the internal cartilage. Cut away the eyes, mouth and innards.

Chop the heads and legs with three of the onions, a clove of garlic and the bacon. Add the parsley and fry the mixture in a tablespoon of olive oil. Add the raw wild rice, and season with salt and pepper.

Use this mixture to stuff the squid. Sew up the ends with thread.

Cooking and serving the squid

Slice the remaining onions. Heat 2 tablespoons of olive oil, add the orange zest and the squid, and brown them lightly. Flame with the brandy, add the white wine, and then add the rest of the garlic, chopped, the herbs, tomato purée and chilli pepper. Cover and simmer for 40 minutes.

Just before serving, remove the squid and keep them hot. Strain the cooking juices and return them to the pan. Away from the heat, stir in the egg yolk and 3 tablespoons of olive oil. Mix together well and taste for seasoning. Heat, but do not allow to boil.

Serve the squid lightly coated with their sauce and sprinkled with chopped parsley.

Suggestions

Choose small squid, which are more tender and have a better flavour than large ones. You could serve the squid with wild rice.

Dublin Bay Prawns with Poached Eggs and Tarragon Vinegar

Langoustines à l'œuf poché et au vinaigre d'estragon

For four people

16 large Dublin Bay prawns
4 eggs
tarragon vinegar, plus 2 sprigs of tarragon from the vinegar
100g *(3½ oz)* butter
3 shallots, finely chopped
4 tomatoes, skinned, deseeded and finely diced
6 tablespoons aromatic white wine *court-bouillon* (p.14)
a dash of red wine vinegar
a pinch of sugar
a dash of olive oil
salt, freshly ground pepper

Preliminary preparations

Shell the raw Dublin Bay prawns (p.102). Reserve the tails in a cool place.

Poach the eggs for 2 minutes in a shallow pan of boiling salted water containing a dash of tarragon vinegar, a sprig of tarragon and some pepper. Remove them to a basin of cold water and reserve.

Making the tarragon-flavoured tomato butter

Sweat the shallots in 20g *(¾ oz)* butter and add the diced tomatoes. Reduce over a low heat to evaporate all the watery juices from the tomatoes. Add the *court-bouillon* and a dash of red wine vinegar and reduce again, by half.

Whisk in most of the remaining butter cut into small pieces. Add the rest of the tarragon leaves, cut into thin shreds. Taste for seasoning and if necessary add a pinch of sugar to lessen the acidity of the tomatoes. Keep hot.

Cooking and serving the Dublin Bay prawns

Heat a nut of butter and a little olive oil in a frying pan and cook the Dublin Bay prawns briefly over a brisk heat. Drain and keep hot.

Put the poached eggs back into their cooking liquid and heat them through. Drain them on kitchen paper.

Place a poached egg in the middle of each of four warmed soup plates. Arrange the Dublin Bay prawns round the sides and coat with the tomato and tarragon butter. Serve at once.

Suggestion
You could add a few tiny dice of bread fried in butter.

Scrambled Eggs with Chicken Livers and Truffles

Œufs brouillés aux foies blonds et aux truffes

For four people

150g *(5½ oz)* pale, firm chicken livers
10 eggs
80g *(3 oz)* butter
1 teaspoon port
1 tablespoon double cream or *crème fraîche* (p.23)
1 tablespoon parsley, chopped
1 teaspoon truffle juice
50g *(2 oz)* truffles, cut into julienne strips
salt, freshly ground pepper

Preliminary preparations
Trim the chicken livers, removing veins and strings. Cut them into small neat dice and reserve.

Break the eggs into a bowl, season them with salt and pepper and add half the butter, cut into small pieces. Whisk lightly with a fork, as if you were making an omelette.

Cooking the chicken livers
Melt a nut of butter in a small non-stick frying pan and brown the diced chicken livers lightly. Season with salt and pepper and deglaze with a dash of port. Set aside.

Cooking the scrambled eggs

Cook the scrambled eggs in the classic way in a heavy pan over a low heat, or in a bain-marie. Stir continuously with a whisk or a wooden spatula until the eggs become thick and creamy. Then add the cream, the remaining butter cut into small pieces and the chopped parsley. Stir in the truffle juice.

Serving the scrambled eggs

Divide the chicken livers between four heated plates and cover immediately with the scrambled eggs. Scatter the julienne of truffles over the top to enhance the look and the flavour of the dish.

Scallops in their Shells

Saint-Jacques à la coque

For four people

8 large scallops in their shells
8 large Dublin Bay prawns

for the **court-bouillon**
half a bottle of dry white wine
1 glass water
1 carrot
1 onion, stuck with a clove
1 *bouquet garni*
1 shallot
1 clove of garlic
1 stick of celery
2 slices of lemon, peeled *à vif*
coarse salt, peppercorns

8 tender asparagus tips, cooked
1 red tomato, skinned, deseeded and cut into dice
150g *(5½ oz)* butter
2 tablespoons double cream or *crème fraîche* (p.23)
a pinch of curry
a pinch of saffron
2 large handfuls of seaweed, blanched
chive tips, sprigs of dill, sprigs of chervil
salt, freshly ground pepper

195

Preliminary preparations

Make the *court-bouillon* by putting all the ingredients together into a stainless-steel or enamelled saucepan and boiling it for 20 minutes. Strain and reserve.

Heat the oven to its highest setting.

Preparing the scallops

Hold each scallop rounded side downwards in the palm of your hand and slide a knife between the two shells, cutting through the scallop where it is attached to the flat upper shell. Detach the top shell carefully. Remove the corals with a small, sharp knife. Slide a table knife beneath the black part near the hinge and remove it, together with the beard which surrounds the white part of the scallop and which is full of sand. Hold the scallop on to the shell with your thumb while you do this. Remove the transparent muscle on the side of the scallop with a teaspoon. The scallop must remain attached to the shell. Wash carefully under cold running water, drain and reserve.

Preparing the Dublin Bay prawns

Shell the tails by twisting the rings in opposite directions to break them. Cut each tail into four pieces to make a *salpicon* and arrange around the scallops on their shells. Scatter tomato dice on top.

Cooking the shellfish

Shortly before serving, arrange the scallops on a baking sheet and cook for about 3 minutes; the time will depend on how hot the oven is. The shellfish will cook together with the tomato. Do not salt them. Test for doneness by pressing the scallops with your fingers, or watch for the juices to run down into the shell.

Finishing the dish

Meanwhile, reheat the asparagus tips in salted water and make the sauce.

Put some of the *court-bouillon* into a small saucepan and whisk in the butter in small pieces to make an emulsified sauce. Add the cream and not too much curry or saffron. Taste for seasoning and adjust the consistency of the sauce.

Divide the seaweed between four heated plates. Arrange two scallops side by side on each plate and decorate with the asparagus tips, placed beside the scallops. Coat lightly with the sauce, which should be a delicate straw colour. Sprinkle with chive tips, chervil and dill.

Suggestions

This dish should look as appealing as it tastes. The scallops, cooked like this, have a particular freshness.

Take care over the timing of the cooking.

If you like, you can make a criss-cross grill pattern on top of the scallops by searing them with a hot iron rod, either before or after they are cooked.

When it comes into contact with the hot scallop shells, the seaweed gives off a delicious smell.

Scallops are in season from October to April. In winter the asparagus tips can be replaced by small wild mushrooms, broccoli or some other green vegetable.

Light Pike Dumplings with Lobster Sauce

Quenelles de brochet mousseline au coulis de homard

For four people

for the dumplings

300g *(10½ oz)* pike, skinned and boned
2 egg whites
300g *(10½ oz)* double cream or *crème fraîche* (p.23)
a pinch of nutmeg
salt, freshly ground pepper

for the lobster sauce

1 lobster, weighing 500–600g *(1 lb 2 oz–1 lb 5 oz)*
20g *(¾ oz)* butter
1 carrot, sliced
1 shallot, chopped
a sprig of thyme
half a bay leaf
a dash of brandy
1 litre *(1¾ pints)* double cream or *crème fraîche* (p.23)
salt, freshly ground pepper, nutmeg

Making the dumpling mixture

Work the pike flesh through a sieve or use the finest blade of a *mouli-légumes*. Transfer it to a bowl placed over crushed ice and allow to chill.

Work in the egg whites, one at a time, with a wooden spatula. Gradually add the cream, season with salt, pepper and nutmeg, and chill for 2–3 hours.

Preparing the lobster sauce

Cook the lobster in boiling salted water for 12–15 minutes. Refresh it under cold running water and shell it.

Cut the flesh into large dice, which will eventually end up in the sauce.

Break up the lobster head shell, removing the gills and inedible parts from inside. Sweat the shells in butter with the vegetables and herbs. Flame with the brandy and add the cream.

Simmer until the sauce becomes velvety and well flavoured. Strain, taste for seasoning, and keep it hot.

Making and cooking the dumplings

Bring a large pan of water to the boil.

Form the dumpling mixture into oval shapes with two wetted soup-spoons. Fill a soup-spoon generously and then smooth the upper side of the mixture into a round by working the spoon against the side of the bowl. With the second spoon dipped in hot water, slide the oval shape into a pan of gently simmering water. Continue until all the mixture is used up; you should have enough for twelve dumplings.

They are cooked when they float to the surface. Using a slotted spoon, transfer them to a bowl of iced water as they rise, and then put them to drain on a cloth.

Finishing and serving the dumplings

Pre-heat the oven to Reg. 6/400°F/200°C.

About 20–25 minutes before serving, slide the *quenelles* into a *gratin* dish and add the diced lobster and halved claws. Coat lightly with the sauce and cook in the oven until the *quenelles* have puffed up.

Serve at once, keeping them covered as you take them to the table.

Suggestions

Like a soufflé, this dish won't wait for the diners to arrive at the table.

Keep the sauce light, fluid and not too strongly flavoured, as it will reduce somewhat in the oven and the dumplings will absorb some of it as they cook.

If you want a more inexpensive dish, you could replace the lobster sauce by a simple *sauce Nantua* – a white wine and cream sauce combined with butter flavoured with the shells and eggs of lobster, crab, crayfish or prawns. It should be a pretty, pale, golden-pink colour.

Lobster Gratin with Oysters

Gratin de homard aux belons

For four people

1–2 lobsters, weighing 1.2kg *(2 lb 10 oz)* altogether
16 oysters
250ml *(8 fl. oz)* shellfish sauce (p.17), prepared with the lobster
  heads and shells
100g *(3½ oz)* butter
1 tablespoon whipped cream
juice of half a lemon
salt, freshly ground pepper

Preparing the lobsters

Cook the lobsters in boiling salted water, allowing 12–20 minutes from the time the water returns to the boil, according to their size. Remove them, refresh them under cold running water and make a hole in the front of the head shell. Stand them tail upwards in a colander to drain, then shell the tails and claws.

Cut the tails into medallions and reserve with the claws, in a cool place. Use the shells to make the shellfish sauce.

Opening the oysters

Open the oysters carefully, filtering their juice into a small saucepan. Heat the grill or a salamander until very hot.

Cooking the lobster and oysters

Just before serving, heat a little butter in a large frying pan and cook the medallions and claws of the lobsters gently to firm them up a little. Add a little of the lobster sauce, heat for a moment, then add a little of the filtered oyster liquid.

Warm the oysters in the rest of their liquid. Arrange the pieces of lobster in one large or, better still, four individual *gratin* dishes.

Finishing and serving the *gratins*

Divide the drained oysters between the four dishes.

Add the whipped cream to the shellfish sauce, tasting it for seasoning and adjusting the consistency. Add a squeeze of lemon juice.

Coat the *gratins* lightly with this sauce and place under the hot grill or salamander. After a few seconds the *gratins* will be glazed to a beautiful golden colour.

Serve at once with fish knives and forks and soup-spoons.

Suggestions

Do not let the oysters actually start to cook.

Use the oyster juice sparingly in the shellfish sauce, as the iodine flavour can be overpowering.

You could combine other shellfish harmoniously with the oysters.

Ravioli
with Chicken Livers and Fresh Truffles

Raviolis de foies blonds aux truffes fraîches

For eight people

for the ravioli dough
215g *(7¹/₂ oz)* plain flour
1 whole egg
1 egg white
1 tablespoon olive oil
1 teaspoon salt
a few drops of water
beaten egg

for the stuffing
4 pale chicken livers
15g *(¹/₂ oz)* butter
1 shallot, chopped
a dash of port
a dash of brandy
150g *(5¹/₂ oz)* chicken liver mousse (p.182)
125ml *(4¹/₂ fl. oz)* double cream or *crème fraîche* (p.23)
20g *(³/₄ oz)* fresh truffles, chopped
salt, freshly ground pepper

for the sauce
125ml *(4¹/₂ fl. oz)* double cream or *crème fraîche* (p.23)
50g *(2 oz)* chicken liver mousse
a dash of port
a dash of vinegar
30g *(1 oz)* fresh truffles, cut into julienne strips
salt, freshly ground pepper

Making the ravioli dough

Sieve the flour into a large bowl, make a well in the centre and add the whole egg, egg white, olive oil and salt. Work them together to form a ball.

Moisten any leftover flour in the bowl with a few drops of water and work into the dough. Knead well and allow to rest, covered, for at least 12 hours.

Making the stuffing

Trim the chicken livers, removing the threads.

Melt a little butter in a frying pan and sauté the livers with the chopped shallot, seasoning them with salt and pepper.

Deglaze the pan with port and brandy and allow to cool.

Purée the livers and chicken liver mousse in a liquidiser or food processor, adding the cream in a thin stream at the end. Taste for seasoning, add the chopped truffles, transfer to a bowl and reserve in a cool place.

Making the ravioli

Divide the dough into two equal parts. Roll out the first one as thinly as possible (if you have a machine it will make this much easier). Sprinkle the dough lightly with flour, if necessary. Brush the surface with beaten egg.

Using a pastry bag or a teaspoon put little mounds of the stuffing in lines, regularly spaced, over the dough.

Roll out the second sheet of dough and place it over the top, sticking the two layers together firmly by pressing round the mounds of filling with your fingertips.

Cut out into ravioli with a special fluted cutter or a knife.

Making the sauce

Reduce the cream slightly in a small pan, then season with salt and pepper. Add the chicken liver mousse at the last moment, together with a dash of port and a few drops of vinegar. Taste for seasoning and strain through a fine wire sieve.

Finishing and serving the ravioli

Cook the ravioli for 3–5 minutes in boiling salted water. Remove with a slotted spoon and divide between four heated plates, or arrange on a serving dish.

Coat lightly with the sauce and scatter the julienne of truffles over the top. Serve at once.

Crying Leg of Lamb

Gigot qui pleure

For six people

1 leg of lamb, weighing 1.6–1.8kg *(3½–4 lb)*
1kg *(2¼ lb)* potatoes
2 cloves of garlic
a sprig of thyme
2 bay leaves
200g *(7 oz)* butter, softened
500ml *(16 fl. oz)* stock or water
butter
salt, freshly ground pepper

Preparing the potatoes

Slice the potatoes very finely – 3mm *(⅛ in)* thick – as if you were making a *gratin*.

Rub a *gratin* dish with the cloves of garlic. Put in the potatoes, overlapping, in layers. Sprinkle with salt, pepper and thyme leaves, add the bay leaves and enough stock or water to come halfway up the potatoes.

Cooking the leg of lamb

Heat the oven to Reg. 9/475°F/240°C and place the *gigot* on a rack above the potatoes. Cover it generously with butter and cook for 15 minutes per lb.

Before carving the lamb, let it rest, covered with aluminium foil, in a warm place for 20 minutes, turning it over twice; it will then be more evenly cooked and tender.

Serving the leg of lamb

Carve the lamb and serve with the delicious potatoes, impregnated with the flavour of the lamb.

Suggestions

In the summer you could make the same dish quite happily with a *gratin* of courgettes, thinly sliced aubergines and skinned, deseeded and diced tomatoes, all lightly moistened with olive oil and seasoned with salt and pepper. In this case, the *gratin* will take somewhat longer to cook.

You could also stick the *gigot* with slivers of garlic and cook it on a spit, with the *gratin* placed underneath.

Cassoulet of Calves' Feet

Pieds de veau en cassoulet

For eight people

4–6 calves' feet, depending on the size, scalded, scraped and split
3 tablespoons olive oil
1 *bouquet garni*
2 carrots, sliced into rounds
1 whole head of garlic, unpeeled
1 onion, stuck with 3 cloves
15–20 black peppercorns
1 tablespoon tomato purée
500g *(1 lb 2 oz)* dried haricot beans, soaked overnight
salt

Cooking the calves' feet

Heat the olive oil in a large, heavy-bottomed saucepan. Sauté the calves' feet gently for a few minutes, without letting them brown, then pour on enough boiling water to cover. Add the *bouquet garni*, carrots, garlic, onion, peppercorns, tomato purée and salt. Skim, then cover and cook at a gentle simmer for 1½ hours.

Adding the beans

After 1½ hours add the beans, cover the pan and simmer for a further 1½ hours, checking from time to time to make sure there is enough liquid in the pan. Remove and bone the calves' feet when they are tender, and return them to the pan. Taste for seasoning.

Serving the cassoulet

Transfer everything to a *gratin* dish and slide under a heated grill for a few minutes, until the top is lightly browned. Serve very hot.

Suggestions

You could use fresh haricot beans (*lingots*), in which case you will need 1kg *(2¼ lb)* in their pods. They will need only 1 hour's cooking time.

This is a very robust winter dish; serve it with a slightly garlic-flavoured salad of frizzy endive.

You could add some salt pork belly at the same time as the beans, or a boiling sausage, 25–30 minutes before the end of the cooking.

Turkey Stuffed with Chestnuts

Dinde de Bresse farcie aux marrons

For eight or ten people

1 free-range turkey, weighing 4kg *(9 lb)*, with its liver
100g *(3¹/₂ oz)* lean veal
100g *(3¹/₂ oz)* pork
100g *(3¹/₂ oz)* green streaky bacon
750g *(1 lb 10 oz)* chestnuts
750ml *(27 fl. oz)* stock
150g *(5¹/₂ oz)* butter
2 shallots, finely chopped
1–2 chopped truffles, with their juice
100g *(3¹/₂ oz)* carrot, onion and shallot, cut into small mirepoix dice
salt, freshly ground pepper

Making the stuffing

Mince or chop the veal, pork and bacon together with the trimmed turkey liver.

Shell and skin the chestnuts (p.176) and cook them in the stock. When they are tender, purée them in a *mouli-légumes* and add them to the meat.

Soften the shallots for a minute in butter and add them to the stuffing with the chopped truffles and their juice. Season well, and the stuffing is ready.

Cooking the turkey

Pre-heat the oven to Reg. 5/375°F/190°C.

Stuff the turkey with the stuffing and tie it up well into a good rounded shape. Put it into a buttered roasting tin or casserole with the mirepoix and coat it liberally in butter.

Season, and roast steadily, basting, for 3 hours. If it starts to get too brown, cover the turkey loosely with aluminium foil.

Finishing and serving the turkey

When it is cooked, transfer the turkey to a large serving dish.

Deglaze the roasting tin with water, strain the sauce and whisk in the remaining butter, cut into small pieces. Sprinkle a little over the turkey.

Serve at once, giving each guest a slice of breast, a bit of leg and some of the stuffing.

Suggestions

Before cooking, it is a good idea to remove the tendons from the legs, having broken the bone just below the drumstick. (Ask your butcher or poulterer to explain how to do this.)

You could accompany this with a small green salad dressed in walnut oil.

Lettuce Loaf

Pain de laitue (pour accompagner les viandes rôties)

2–3 handsome lettuces
1 litre *(1¾ pints)* rather thick classic béchamel sauce
2 eggs
50g *(2 oz)* butter
50g *(2 oz)* fine pale breadcrumbs
salt, pepper and nutmeg

Preparing the lettuce

Remove the dark green outside leaves of the lettuces and cut away their thick stalks with a small sharp knife. Blanch the leaves for a few minutes in boiling salted water, then drain them well and chop them finely in a food processor.

Stir the lettuce into the béchamel sauce, together with the eggs. Taste for seasoning, adding salt, pepper and nutmeg; you should have a very smooth mixture.

Cooking the 'loaf'

Pre-heat the oven to Reg. 2/300°F/150°.

Butter the inside of a charlotte mould and dust it with the fine breadcrumbs. Pour in the lettuce mixture and cook in a bain-marie for about an hour. Turn out just before serving.

Suggestions

This homely recipe, taken from my grandmother's hand-written recipe book, should be served with roast beef, roast pork or roast veal. Sprinkle the loaf with the juices from the meat.

Grenadines of Veal with Salsify and Ginger

Grenadins de veau aux salsifis et au gingembre

For four people

800g *(1¾ lb)* fillet of veal, cut into 8 medallions
1kg *(2¼ lb)* salsify
1 lemon
1 tablespoon flour
150g *(5½ oz)* butter
a piece of fresh ginger 4cm *(1½ in)* square
2 tablespoons parsley, chopped
100ml *(4 fl. oz)* dry white wine
3 tablespoons meat glaze or concentrated veal stock
500ml *(16 fl. oz)* double cream or *crème fraîche* (p.23)
salt, freshly ground pepper

Preliminary preparations

Peel the salsify, squeeze lemon juice over them and cut them into sticks 6–7cm *(2½ in)* long. Cook them in a large pan of salted water with a tablespoon of flour in it for about 2 hours. Keep an eye on them, and when they are tender drain and reserve.

Flatten the medallions of veal slightly with a cutlet beater or large, heavy knife blade.

Peel the ginger, cut it into julienne strips, and blanch in simmering water for 5 minutes; drain and repeat with fresh water.

Cooking the veal

Brown the pieces of veal in butter in a sauté pan. When they have browned, turn down the heat and cook gently for 10 minutes. Drain and keep hot.

Finishing and serving the veal and salsify

Sauté the salsify in butter in a large sauté pan until they are lightly browned. Sprinkle them with parsley and keep hot.

Deglaze the pan in which the veal was cooked with the white wine. Add the stock or meat glaze.

Strain the sauce into a pan and add the ginger and the cream. Reduce until the sauce is velvety.

Taste for seasoning and serve the veal on four heated plates, lightly coated with the sauce, and with the drained salsify arranged next to it.

Potée of Pigeons, Guinea Fowl and Chicken with Vegetables

Potée bressane aux trois volailles

For eight people

3 farmed pigeons
1 free-range guinea fowl, weighing about 1.5kg *(3 lb 2 oz)*
1 free-range chicken, weighing about 1.8kg *(4 lb)*
1kg *(2¼ lb)* carrots, peeled
4–5 leeks, cleaned
2 onions, stuck with 4 cloves
1 *bouquet garni*
500g *(1 lb 2 oz)* turnips, peeled
100g *(3½ oz)* celery stalks
10 waxy potatoes
1 Savoy cabbage
salt, freshly ground pepper

Making the *bouillon*

Put all the necks, wings, feet, etc., from the poultry into a large saucepan with two carrots, the green leaves of the leeks, the onions and the *bouquet garni*. Bring to the boil, skim and simmer for 1 hour.

Remove the poultry trimmings, herbs and vegetables with a skimmer. Season carefully.

Poaching the poultry

Poach the chicken and the guinea fowl first. Let them cook gently for 15 minutes, then skim the *bouillon* meticulously.

Add the remaining carrots and the turnips and cook for a further 15 minutes. Add the sticks of celery and the leeks, and skim again.

When the poultry has cooked for 45 minutes add the pigeons and cook for a further half an hour.

Meanwhile, cook the potatoes and cabbage separately, making sure they are not overcooked.

Finishing and serving the dish

After a total cooking time of 1 hour 15 minutes, test the birds and vegetables to see if they are ready.

207

Carve the birds and arrange them on a large serving dish with their vegetables on a second dish. Give each guest some of the three different sorts of poultry; serve in soup plates with the vegetables and some of the *bouillon*, strained and tasted for seasoning.

Suggestions

This wonderful peasant dish is almost a meal in itself. You could enhance the flavour of the stock with a dash of olive oil or walnut oil and a few drops of vinegar.

Scallops with Mussels and Chicory

Coquilles Saint-Jacques aux moules, aux endives et au vinaigre

For four people

12 large scallops
500g *(1 lb 2 oz)* mussels
4 heads of chicory
100g *(3½ oz)* butter
juice of half a lemon
2 shallots, chopped
200ml *(7 fl. oz)* dry white wine
500ml *(16 fl. oz)* rose pink sauce (p.22)
salt, freshly ground pepper

Preliminary preparations

Clean the scallops, keeping only the white parts. Cut them in half horizontally if they are very large. Reserve them in a cool place.

Scrub and scrape the mussels, trimming their beards.

Stew the chicory in a covered pan with a little water, a generous nut of butter and a squeeze of lemon juice. When the chicory is tender, keep it hot.

Cooking the mussels

Cook the mussels as you would if you were making *moules marinière*, by softening the shallots in butter and adding the white wine, then cooking the mussels in this liquid, in a covered pan, until they have all opened. Remove them with a slotted spoon and take them out of their shells. Keep them warm in a small bowl. Reserve their cooking liquid.

208

Making the rose pink sauce

Filter the mussels' cooking liquid through a cloth and use it to make the rose pink sauce.

Finishing and serving the dish

When you are ready to serve the scallops, sauté them in butter for 2–3 minutes in a frying pan.

Arrange the chicory, well drained and cut into rounds 1cm (*½ in*) thick, in the centre of four heated plates. Arrange the scallops and mussels alternately round the chicory. Coat lightly with the rose pink sauce and serve at once.

Suggestions

You could cook the scallops on a buttered baking sheet in the oven.

The mussels could be replaced by oysters.

Steamed Truffled Chicken with Cream

Poularde de Bresse truffée cuite à la vapeur

For four people

1 plump free-range chicken, weighing 1.8–2kg *(4–4½ lb)*, with its liver
3–4 truffles
80g *(3 oz)* butter
2 dashes of Armagnac, Marc de Bugey or other marc
1½ litres *(2½ pints)* good chicken stock
200ml *(7 fl. oz)* dry white wine
1 *bouquet garni*
2 sticks of celery
2 carrots, coarsely sliced
1 onion
a nut of *beurre manié*
200ml *(7 fl. oz)* thick double cream
1 egg yolk
juice of half a lemon
salt, freshly ground pepper

Preparing the chicken (3–4 hours ahead)

Slice one or two of the truffles and slide the round slices under the skin covering the breast of the chicken.

209

Chop the remaining truffles and the chicken liver and sauté them briefly in butter. Season the mixture with salt and pepper and sprinkle with Armagnac or marc.

Put this stuffing inside the chicken, wrap it in a cloth and let it sit in a cool place for several hours to absorb the flavour of the truffles.

Cooking the chicken

Put the stock, white wine, *bouquet garni* and vegetables in the bottom of the pan, then put a colander or sieve (or use a *couscoussier* or large steamer) on top. Add a dash of Armagnac.

Put the chicken in the colander or steamer – the liquid should not touch it. Cover the pan hermetically and steam for 1¼–1½ hours.

Finishing and serving the chicken

At the end of the cooking time, remove the chicken and keep it hot.

Reduce the cooking liquid somewhat, then thicken it slightly with *beurre manié*. Strain it through a fine sieve and, away from the heat, add the cream mixed with the egg yolk. Taste for seasoning and add a little lemon juice. Heat without allowing it to boil.

Carve the chicken in front of the guests and serve the sauce separately. Do not forget the stuffing.

Suggestions

You could serve this dish with wild rice cooked in chicken stock.

Test the chicken to see if it is done by piercing the thigh with a carving fork.

Saddle of Hare with Caramelised Apples, Celeriac and Golden Sauce

Râble de lièvre aux pommes caramélisées et au céleri sauce blonde

For two people

1 saddle of hare
1 carrot, sliced
1 onion, coarsely chopped
2 shallots, coarsely chopped
half a lemon, peeled *à vif* and sliced
a sprig of thyme
1 bay leaf
several peppercorns and juniper berries
100ml *(4 fl. oz)* olive oil
1 celeriac, peeled and diced
1 glass of milk
2 apples (russets or Golden Delicious)
100g *(3½ oz)* butter
100ml *(4 fl. oz)* dry white wine
250ml *(8 fl. oz)* double cream or *crème fraîche* (p.23)
1–2 tablespoons civet sauce (optional)
a dash of lemon juice or vinegar
salt, freshly ground pepper

Marinating the saddle of hare (one day ahead)

The saddle is the part of the animal between the beginning of the neck and the tail. (Use the forelegs and hindlegs to make a civet or a game pâté.)

Remove the thin membrane that covers the saddle, using a small sharp knife. Put the saddle into a small, deep dish which just fits it, together with the carrot, onion, shallots, lemon, herbs and spices. Add any trimmings from the hare, cover it completely with olive oil and let it marinate in the refrigerator for 24 hours.

Cooking the celeriac purée

Put the celeriac into a saucepan of water together with a glass of milk. Cook for about 1 hour, then drain and work through a sieve or purée in a *mouli-légumes*.

Add a nut of butter, a little cream, and the civet sauce if using it, and season well. Keep hot in a bain-marie.

Cooking the saddle of hare

Heat the oven to its highest setting.

Take the saddle out of its marinade and put it into a small roasting tin with a little olive oil. Brown it all over, then add the strained vegetables, trimmings and seasonings from the marinade. Roast it for 8–10 minutes, turning and basting frequently.

Cooking the apples

While the hare is cooking, peel and core the apples and cut each into ten slices. Cook them in butter in a medium frying pan, turning them from time to time. Keep hot.

Finishing and serving the saddle

When the saddle is cooked, but still pink inside, transfer it to a dish and cover it with aluminium foil. Keep it hot.

Skim the roasting tin and deglaze it with the white wine, boiling it rapidly until it has almost evaporated.

Add the rest of the cream and let it reduce, with all the vegetables and seasonings, until it is an amber colour, shiny, velvety and well flavoured. Strain it through a fine sieve and finish it by whisking in a little butter, and adding a dash of lemon juice or vinegar, or even a little of the olive oil from the marinade.

Remove the fillets from the roasted saddle and slice them. Arrange them on two large heated plates with a spoonful of celeriac purée and the caramelised apples placed next to the slices of saddle. Coat lightly with the golden sauce and serve at once.

Spit-roasted Capon
with a Gratin of Cardoons

Chapon de Bresse à la broche gratin de cardons à la moelle

For eight people

1 large free-range capon, weighing 3½–4½kg *(8–10 lb)*
1 cardoon
a dash of vinegar
3 tablespoons flour
juice of half a lemon
200g *(7 oz)* butter
2 shallots, finely chopped
1 litre *(1¾ pints)* chicken stock
5–6 marrow bones, cut in half
salt, freshly ground pepper

Preparing the cardoon

Remove the coarse or wilted outside leaves of the cardoon. Cut those that are tender into even slices 5–8cm *(2–3 in)* long. Remove all the stringy fibres from each one. Reserve them in cold water acidulated with vinegar, or rub them with half a lemon, to prevent them from blackening.

Cooking the cardoon

Prepare a *blanc* by mixing 1 tablespoon of flour into a large saucepan of water. Bring to the boil, add the juice of half a lemon and season with salt and pepper. Put in the cardoon and cook, covered, for 1½–2 hours, stirring often to prevent it sticking to the bottom of the pan. Test frequently, and when it is tender drain and reserve.

Cooking the capon

Season the cleaned, trussed capon inside with salt and pepper, then spread it with a little butter. Put it on to the spit (or just roast it in the oven in the ordinary way). Cook it briskly to begin with and then with a moderate heat. Baste it often with its own juices.

Making the velouté sauce

Soften the shallots in some of the fat that comes off the chicken as it cooks. Stir in 1–2 tablespoons of flour, let it cook for a few moments, then gradually add the chicken stock. Leave to simmer for half an hour.

Preparing the marrow

Remove the marrow in cylinders from the bones and cut it into rounds 1cm *(½ in)* thick.

Heat the oven to its highest setting.

Cooking the cardoon *gratin*

Put the cooked cardoon in a large *gratin* dish, interspersing with the rounds of marrow. Pour the velouté sauce over the top. Put into the oven to cook and brown on the top.

Finishing and serving the capon

To test the capon, prick the thick part of the thigh with a needle (when it is done, the juices will run clear without any trace of blood). It should be very succulent.

Carve it and divide it between eight heated plates, giving each guest a piece of thigh and a slice of breast. Serve it with the *gratin* of cardoon.

Suggestions

This dish, which makes a good feast for Christmas or New Year, could be accompanied by a mixed salad of chicory, frizzy endive and raddicchio, dressed with walnut oil.

Light Chocolate Mousse

Mousse légère au chocolat

For eight people

10 eggs
200–250g *(7–8¹/₂ oz)* dark chocolate (eating chocolate)
a pinch of salt

Separate the eggs, putting the whites in a bowl large enough to whisk them to a meringue later.

Break up the chocolate and melt it in the top half of a double boiler.

Away from the heat, incorporate the egg yolks, one at a time, stirring lightly with a wooden spoon until you have a smooth mixture.

Whisk the egg whites to a fairly firm snow, adding a pinch of salt at the beginning.

Pour in the chocolate mixture, folding it in lightly but thoroughly with a wooden spatula.

Transfer the mixture to a serving bowl and keep in the refrigerator until you wish to serve the mousse.

Suggestions

The texture of the egg whites is very important; take care that they do not become grainy.

Serve with slices of brioche.

Crystallised Pink Grapefruit Peel

Ecorces de pamplemousses roses confites

Preliminary preparations

Take very large pink grapefruit and, using a filleting knife or other sharp supple knife, cut away the base of each one so that it will stand quite steadily on a board.

Make several vertical incisions all round the grapefruit to divide the peel into sections. Remove the peel.

With the insides of the grapefruit, make a fruit salad by cutting the segments *à vif* (slicing against the inner membranes so that each segment comes out 'naked' and free of skin and membranes). Put them in a salad bowl and sprinkle with sugar.

Cut the peel into long strips the size of a *pomme frite* (narrower than a chip). Blanch them three times, starting with cold water each time and allowing them to cook for 5 minutes at a rapid boil.

Drain and weigh the peel, then put it into a saucepan with an equal weight of sugar. Add a little water to help melt the sugar.

Gradually raise the heat until the syrup is boiling, then turn it down to a simmer and cook for 30 minutes.

When they become transparent, remove the pieces of peel with a slotted spoon and leave on a rack to drain. Roll them in granulated sugar when they have cooled and dried somewhat, and serve with petit fours and other little delicacies at the end of a meal.

Suggestions

Keep in a cool place.

Mère Blanc's Vonnas Pancakes

Crêpes de 'la mère Blanc'

For six people

500g *(1 lb 2 oz)* potatoes, peeled
3 tablespoons milk
3 tablespoons flour
3 whole eggs
4 egg whites
3 tablespoons double cream
400g *(14 oz)* clarified butter or oil for frying

Making the pancake batter

Cook the potatoes in boiling salted water, drain them well and make a purée, adding a little milk.

Allow to cool in a large bowl, then gradually mix in the flour, and then the eggs, one at a time, and the unbeaten egg whites.

Gradually add the cream and stir; you should have a fairly thick batter (which can be made thinner, if necessary, after trying out one pancake.) Do not beat the batter too hard.

Frying the pancakes

Take a large steel pan and put in as much clarified butter, or oil, as you would if you were making an omelette. Heat over a brisk heat and pour in ¾ tablespoon of the mixture. The mixture will form a round almost like a fritter.

You can make 6–7 pancakes at once. They cook very quickly; turn each one with a metal spatula as it cooks.

When they are cooked through and light brown on both sides, pile them into a serving dish and serve very hot.

Suggestions

The potato purée or the batter itself can be made the day before. Keep it in the refrigerator, but let it come slowly back to room temperature before using it.

These are Mère Blanc's famous Vonnas pancakes, which can be eaten either sprinkled with salt as an accompaniment to meat, or with sugar or cinnamon as a dessert.

Coffee Parfait

Parfait au moka

For eight people

250ml *(8 fl. oz)* water
200g *(7 oz)* caster sugar
8 egg yolks
750ml *(27 fl. oz)* whipping cream, whipped
150ml *(5 fl. oz)* very strong coffee

Dissolve the sugar in the water in a medium saucepan and bring it to the boil. Allow to cool.

Put the egg yolks in a basin with this syrup and place over a bain-marie of simmering water. Whisk until the mixture becomes light and creamy.

217

Remove from the heat, put the basin over a bowl of cracked ice, and whisk until completely cold.

Fold in the whipped cream and the coffee.

Fill eight coffee cups with the mixture and chill for at least 3 hours.

Four-fruit Cocktail Sorbet

Sorbet cocktail aux quatre fruits

850g *(1 lb 14 oz)* caster sugar
1 litre *(1¾ pints)* water
1 vanilla pod, split lengthwise
6 lemons
12 large juicy oranges
1 ripe pineapple
2 ripe bananas
a dash of grenadine

Make the syrup by dissolving the sugar in the water with the vanilla pod and bringing it to the boil. Stir and then allow to cool.

Squeeze the juice from the lemons and oranges.

Peel, quarter and core the pineapple, then cut it into small pieces. Purée the pineapple and the bananas in a *mouli-légumes*.

Mix the four fruits together. Colour the syrup with a dash of grenadine and mix it into the fruit purée. Freeze in a sorbet-maker and keep in the freezer.

This is an excellent sorbet for winter when there is no soft fruit to be had.

Suggestions
The acidity of the citrus fruits is mellowed by the pineapple and bananas.

The sweetness of the syrup can be adjusted according to your own taste; the sorbet should be neither too sharp nor too sweet.

The sorbet can be served on its own or with a fruit salad.

Serve with little butter biscuits (*sablés au beurre*) cooked shortly before they are needed.

Chocolate Tart

Tarte au chocolat

For four people

for the tart
125g *(4½ oz)* dark eating chocolate
100g *(3½ oz)* good butter, unsalted
50g *(2 oz)* flour
150g *(5½ oz)* caster sugar
4 eggs

for the icing
100g *(3½ oz)* bitter cooking chocolate or dark eating chocolate
4½ tablespoons whipping cream
20g *(¾ oz)* butter
unsweetened cocoa powder

Making the tart

Melt the chocolate, broken into pieces, and the butter, in the top of a bain-marie.

In a separate bowl, mix the flour with the sugar and eggs. Stir in the melted chocolate and butter mixture and mix for 10 minutes with a wooden spatula. When the mixture is very smooth and makes a ribbon, transfer it to a buttered tart tin or sponge tin. The tart should be no more than 3cm *(1¼ in)* deep.

Pre-heat the oven to Reg. 6/400°F/200°C.

Cook the tart for 30 minutes. Test by piercing with a small knife; it will come out clean when the tart is cooked. Turn out upside down on a cake rack and allow to cool.

Making the icing

Melt the chocolate, broken into pieces, and the butter in the top of a bain-marie.

Bring the cream to the boil and add it to the chocolate, mixing well until the mixture is shiny and smooth.

Coat the top and sides of the tart with this mixture. Allow to set a little and then make a criss-cross pattern on the top with the back of a large knife. Sprinkle with cocoa powder and serve.

Suggestions

The same tart could be served on its own, without the icing and simply powdered with icing sugar. This makes it into a more rustic dish.

219

Lemon Tart

Tarte au citron

For eight people

for the flan pastry

300g *(10¹/₂ oz)* flour, sifted
150g *(5¹/₂ oz)* butter, softened
150g *(5¹/₂ oz)* icing sugar
2 eggs

for the lemon cream

3 lemons
150g *(5¹/₂ oz)* caster sugar
150ml *(¹/₄ pint)* double cream or *crème fraîche* (p.23)
2 eggs
2 dessertspoons rum

Making the flan pastry

Work the softened butter and icing sugar together in a bowl. Add the eggs and then work in the sifted flour. Let it rest for several hours before use.

Preparing the lemon cream

Wash the lemons and grate the zest into a basin. Add the sugar, cream, eggs and rum.

Cooking the flan

Pre-heat the oven to Reg. 6/400°F/200°C.

Roll out the pastry, line a tart tin, prick it and bake it blind to a pale golden brown.

Reduce the heat to Reg. 4/350°F/180°C. Pour in the cream and cook for a further 15–18 minutes.

A few minutes before the end of the cooking, peel the lemons *à vif* and cut them into thin slices. Arrange the slices prettily on top of the tart and sprinkle it with icing sugar when it cools. Serve cold.

Orange Charlotte

Charlotte à l'orange

For four people

6 medium oranges (preferably blood oranges)
300g *(10 oz)* caster sugar
200ml *(7 fl. oz)* whipping cream
4 leaves of gelatine

Lining the charlotte mould

You will need a straight-sided mould 15cm *(6 in)* across and 5cm *(2 in)* high.

Slice two oranges into very thin slices, 2–3mm *(⅛ in)* thick. Put them into a saucepan, cover them with water, bring them to the boil, then drain and allow them to cool.

Repeat this operation twice more, then add 200g *(7 oz)* sugar and 200ml *(7 fl. oz)* water. Bring to the boil and simmer very gently for an hour, making sure that the syrup does not evaporate too much, and adding a little more water if necessary.

When the oranges are cooked (test by squeezing one between your finger and thumb; it should be tender and supple), drain carefully and set aside to cool.

Butter the inside of the mould and sprinkle it with sugar, then line it with slices of orange. Chill in the refrigerator.

Making the orange mousse

Put the cream into a large bowl and whisk until fairly firm. Reserve in the refrigerator.

Grate the zest of two oranges into a sauté pan. Add their juice and 80g *(3 oz)* sugar. Bring to the boil and reduce by half.

Soften the leaves of gelatine in a bowl of cold water, drain them and add them to the orange syrup, away from the heat, whisking to help them dissolve. Add the juice of the two remaining oranges.

Chill in the refrigerator until the mixture starts to thicken, stirring from time to time to prevent lumps forming.

Add the cream to the mixture, folding it in very thoroughly.

Fill the prepared mould with this mixture and chill in the refrigerator for at least 2 hours before serving. Turn out the charlotte after dipping the mould briefly into hot water.

Suggestions

You could line the mould with lady finger biscuits or fine slices of home-made Swiss roll filled with Seville marmalade or raspberry or strawberry jam.

This dessert can be served with an orange salad sprinkled with Grand Marnier.

Index

226